**S&B RANCH PUBLISHING
PRESENTS**

A HERE EVER AFTER PRODUCTION

ANGELS AND OUTLAWS

BY WILLIAM J. CHAMBERS MSed.

First Edition

Production Manager: Susan R. Hairrell

Edited by Sherri Watson & Glory Ann Kurtz

S&B Ranch Publishing
P.O. Box 1338
Boyd Texas 76023

**COPYRIGHT BY WILLIAM J. CHAMBERS MSed.
2014 - All Rights Reserved**

*Cover design by Aysha Hoffman.
Cover painting by Karen Kennedy Chatham*

DEDICATION

Every time I write a book I save the dedication until the last. This year isn't any different. What is different about this year is I thought about the dedication the whole time I was working on this book. I usually save this section for someone who has passed on. This year that was almost me, and I am not ready to write that one yet.

This year I saved this special to honor the living. More importantly to honor those who made sure I was still living. I dedicate this book to the doctors and nurses at Harris Hospital in Fort Worth. I know I wasn't a model patient, so thank you all for putting up with me and giving me back to all those who love me.

I dedicate this book to my friends who have become like family to me. I thank you from the bottom of my heart to all those who sent up prayers to the Master. I dedicate this to Jon and JJ for taking care of me until I could take care of myself. To Susan and Sherri who always kept my spirits up and to all of you just for loving me.

I dedicate this book to my music family, who gave me one hell of a party. Thank you all. It will be a night I will always remember. Also, this book is dedicated to all those who attended; to those who brought and bought items in the auction.

Lastly this book is dedicated to the best neighbors on planet earth. I am blessed to live next door to the Saint of Cottondale, his wife Emily, Jeremy and his wife Patty from just down the road.

TABLE OF CONTENTS

Chapter 1	INTRODUCTION
Chapter 2	THE CALM BEFORE THE STORM
Chapter 3	INTO THE DARKNESS
Chapter 4	MEANWHILE BACK AT THE RANCH
Chapter 5	ESCAPE FROM ICU
Chapter 6	I WANT TO GO BACK TO MY HORSE STALL
Chapter 7	WILD BILL'S UNFORGETABLE ADVENTURE
Chapter 8	AT THE DOUBLE J RANCH
Chapter 9	HOMECOMING
Chapter 10	A BIG BALL IN COWTOWN
Chapter 11	FULL CIRCLE

INTRODUCTION

To tell you all the truth, this is not the book I was going to write this year. I had in mind to write another children's book. I had it more than just on my mind; I had the thing about halfway done. But then suddenly life happened and it made a big splash when it did.

I never intended to write a book like this at all. Then on May 3, my life was nearly lost. Having a near-death experience is enough to cause a person to rethink things. I put the children's book on the shelf until further notice. Maybe I'll save it for next year.

This is not my typical Wild Bill, rodeo cowboy, light-hearted book. All my books come from the heart; it's just the way I write. Mike Blakely once said, "I lived it before I wrote it." It is so true. That's just the way I write. I live it inside my head before I write a single word. This book not only comes from my heart but also comes from my soul.

This year my book is a little different. I actually really did live this book. Believe me, I have the scars and the hospital bills to prove it. What I have more than anything else is the insight to write it. Certain insight isn't easily obtained and it's time consuming. It took a major automobile wreck and three months to gain the insight I never had before.

Friends, I can honestly say I am not sorry it happened. What's that they say, "What doesn't kill you makes you stronger." That is sure enough a fact. Once I learned how fragile life truly was, I began to be a lot more grateful.

I also learned you don't have to be related to be family. The friendships I share with so many are just as good as being related by blood. I can't tell you how many prayers went up for me. I will never know, only the good Lord has that score. But I do know they did work because I am here today and I shouldn't be. The way everyone reached out to me, taught me the greatest lesson of all: I am loved and loved by many.

This book tells the story about the past three months of my life. It's about the friends who made this remarkable journey with me, and how they kept my spirits up. It is for them that I share this story. Hopefully this story will make you both laugh and cry. I know it did me.

About the only thing left to say is thank for your support through this summer and through the years. It has been a hell of a ride, but I ain't done yet. I have a book or two and a million miles left in these old bones.

CHAPTER 1

THE CALM BEFORE THE STORM

By now most of you know how I started my summer. It was not the start I was hoping for, not by any means. The summers are the busy time of year for this cowboy scribe. They are filled with rodeos, horse shows, cuttings and ropings. It just wasn't meant to be this year.

This is my first stab at non-fiction since a little book called **Horse Sense**. I don't know if that book was non-fiction or just an educated cowboy's opinion. At any rate, you good people seemed to like it.

This book has nothing at all to do with my opinion and everything to do with you. Because when everything was said and done, it was your prayers and support that helped me survive not an endless summer but my never-ending summer. You, the readers and you my dear friends inspire me and inspired this book.

It all started on April 30. I got up early that morning to get ready to go peddle my books at a three-day roping. I remember looking at myself in the mirror that morning as I shaved. For the first time I saw myself as a successful author.

Now don't get me wrong, writing hadn't made me rich but it has afforded me the life I always wanted. I have a little ranch and all kinds of critters. My seventeen novels kept the mortgage paid, everybody fed and my truck running up and going down the highway. To a cowboy, that's pretty much a success, or so I thought.

It wasn't long before I had my animals fed and my truck loaded for a three-day cruise. I didn't know then but like Gilligan, I got a little lost. But there I go getting ahead of myself and the story.

It's about ninety miles from my place to Hamilton, Texas. Hamilton was the site of one of the largest ropings in the Lone Star State this year. I just knew I had to be there.

It seems I am always going on the weekends in the late spring and early summer. So you might say I put in a lot of windshield time going here and there from one event to the next. I usually start my trips talking a bit with the Good Lord.

I like to tell Him each day how grateful I am because my life has been truly blessed. You see I wasn't supposed to live but a few hours after my birth. When the powers that be saw I was going to make it, their thought was I would never walk or talk and I would definitely be retarded. Well I never shut up, I walk more than most my age and I do have a few degrees. So much for the powers that be!

When I was about 17, I found this neat substance called beer. It made me feel like I was just like everybody else. I went from being a crippled cowboy to being a drunken-ass crippled cowboy. Ten years later, I was a hopeless drunk. Once again the powers that be stepped in and told my mother unless she put me away, I was going to die - and soon.

It has been nearly thirty years since I had my last drink. Since then I have finished my education and settled into my writing career. I'm not telling you this in a boastful way but because I know it was someone a whole lot bigger than me who has always saved me - from birth, from myself and from a couple of dumb-ass kids joyriding one Sunday afternoon.

The last fifteen years has been the best part of my life. I have proven myself in the horse world as a writer. I met and grew close to my idol Chris LeDoux. I honored the man at his passing with three novels taken from his songs. I have seen this beautiful country, from Canada to Mississippi, all on an endless book tour.

And friends, let me tell you that I have met the best in the world: from millionaires to a grumpy old horse trainer named Bob Kurtz. I miss Bob every day. And then there is the family that has adopted me: Susan, Ty, Brandon and Tyla, and the whole Rogers clan.

I say all of this so you know why I have to tell the Good Lord every day, usually driving down the road, just how grateful I am. Because without his blessings, my life would have been over before it ever started.

That's one way of looking at it; another is the Good Lord is about the only one brave enough to ride with me. So I might as well talk to Him. It does make the windshield time pass.

With all I had to be grateful for, my conversation with the man upstairs took every bit of 45 minutes. By then I had passed through Weatherford. When my little prayer was over, I began thinking about the upcoming week.

My good friend and notable horse trainer, Bozo Rogers had found me an old gelding up on the Waggoner Ranch. The plan was to go get him as soon as I had a barn built, which was to be the week following the roping. So in my head, I was either building a barn or riding my new horse. I must say when it comes to horses, I am like a little boy again but you will learn that about me as you read.

The next thing I knew, I was entering Glen Rose. It occurred to me that I had yet to deliver my newest book to the library in this small town that I knew so well. I thought there was no time like the present, so I left the main road and made my delivery.

It had been over a year since I had been to the library but when I walked in, it felt like I had been there just the day before. The same two ladies who have greeted me for years were there once more. I must say they are some of the sweetest you'll ever find. As always they met me with hugs at the door.

Thirty minutes later, I was back on my way to Hamilton and the roping. Once again my mind was on either building a barn or riding my new gelding. I am sure a small prayer crossed my lips, like "Lord, help me do a good job today."

I was entering the gate of the arena before I knew it. They said it was going to be big, I just didn't know how big until I arrived. There must have been a thousand trucks and trailers from all over the South and the Southwest.

"Now this is my kind of party," I remember thinking.

With all the folks roping and since ropers are not known for their parking skills, it took a while to find a parking spot. I didn't mind, I am not the greatest at parking either. Perhaps that is why I fit in with them so well. It wasn't long before I had my rig parked just as haphazard as any roper there. If you didn't know me, you might think I was there to rope.

When I first started years ago, I walked the parking lots, barns, and arenas selling my books. I walked many a mile at every horse event you can think of. I was a younger man back then. A few years back, I swallowed my pride and got me a Hoveround thingamajig. I was 54 soon to be 55. Hurt pride is a lot easier to get over than hurt feet.

I kept this motorized easy chair in the back of my SUV. Now this thing weighs about a 150 pounds. It takes two ropers to unload the thing. Since I am not a roper, I had to find two. The first thing I learned about ropers was that despite their lack of parking skills, they are good people. Help is never hard to find.

Before long we had my step saver unloaded, my book bag filled with my latest creation and I was ready to start my day.

I have been doing ropings for a long time and over the years I have gotten to know a lot of these modern day cowboys. But these huge ropings are a cat of a different stripe. If I was lucky, I might know half of them. But me being me, I have never met a stranger. So off I went.

I made my first sale minutes after leaving my truck, then another and another. My books fell like dominos. Before I knew it 20 were gone. That got me to thinking, what if I wasn't the only one at this roping.

Hamilton is not that big of a city and because of the roping, the population more than likely doubled. With the influx in the population and the known fact that the town only had three motels, I thought to myself that I ought to stop pushing paper and secure myself some lodging for the evening.

Of the three motels in Hamilton, two were older than dirt. Davy Crockett probably stayed at one on his way to the Alamo. But one was brand new and at the arena. The new one was my first stop.

It was clean and downright beautiful. But if I have learned nothing else from the ladies, I have learned beauty is not cheap. The deal was I had to stay two nights at $170 a night. I am thinking to myself, "They do realize I wasn't trying to buy the joint".

You know where I slept that night and the next night. If it was good enough for Davy, it would suit me fine," I told myself. Perhaps if I knew then what I know now, I might have treated myself to the fancy digs.

Once I had my lodging secured for the weekend, it was time for a bite to eat before returning to the event. By the time I arrived back at the arena, the roping was nearly completed for the day. That meant it was prime pickings for me.

This is late in the afternoon when folks are pitching camp, sitting outside of their living quarters or sharing a brew and a story with friends. It's almost like I have a captured audience.

I heard more than once, "Hey Bill, you want a beer?" After all these years of doing these kinds of events, I have a pretty standard answer. "That's alright, I don't need beer to walk funny," is my usual come back.

But every now and then you have some yea-who with a wiser crack than I had been getting away with for years. I guess it was just that time.

"Hey Bill, come on have a beer. Who knows it might make you walk better," some knucklehead called out.

I thought about my next words and chose them carefully. "Well son, I tested that theory for the best part of a decade in my youth, and it just didn't have that affect on me. Believe me son, I tested it about every way it could be tested," I fired back.

Everybody had a good laugh, especially when I added, "There's more than one way to be quick on your feet." It always feels good to get one up on the peanut gallery.

All in all, it was a pretty good first day. I saw some old friends, made some new ones, shared a laugh or two and sold nearly a box of books. That was a pretty good start for a three-day roping.

The next morning I awoke to a sunny day. I said a prayer, got dressed and had a bite to eat. That is when I had an Idea. I was going to be at the arena all day so why should I rush it? I decided to run down to the John Deere house and see the owner.

I had met Billy years earlier when I was touring with my book *Horse Sense*. He liked the book so well that he ordered a dozen more. The next year I bought a mower from him and we've been friends ever since. So why not go chew the fat with Billy while I was in town.

I found my friend busy as usual but he took the time to talk to me. I told him he should sell the dealership and build a motel since they were in short supply. He laughed like he knew what I was getting at. Before long the visit was over and we both headed out. But that was not the last time I saw Billy. I ran into him twice more that day.

The first thing I had to do when I got to the arena was round up the Hoveround. I had left it charging at a friend's campsite. With all the new arrivals, the trick would be to find its location. You take five or six hundred trucks and trailers and you turn a parking lot into a maze. Like a rat, I searched until I found my faithful mount.

It took a while but by 10 a.m., I was saddled up and ready to push a little paper. Up one row I went and down the next. One book sold then two. After an hour I had one left in my book bag. I spied this fellow just getting out of his truck. It looked like the perfect home for my last book, and it was.

I found out he was from Van Zandt County. Wills Point is in Van Zandt County as well as being the home of one of my oldest friends. His name is Bobby Deane. You might recognize the name because his name has appeared in many of my novels.

Bobby first appeared as the old horse trainer in **The Yellow Outlaw Stud**, the very first of my Chris LeDoux-inspired novels. He then was in *Old Songs and Memories,* the last in the trilogy. Matter of fact, he was in my last book as well as my newest books, **The Spur and the Prickly Pear** and *The Lord of the Arenas*, which was the book the man had just bought.

In the newest book Bobby appears as the wayward prince from the Kingdom of Texas. Bobby is not the only friend who has appeared in my novels. The reason I do this is to honor my dear friends, for they mean the world to me.

Come to find out, this man who bought my book knew Bobby. So we spent the next twenty minutes telling Bobby Deane stories. Texas might be a large state, but it's a small world.

Just talking to the fellow got me to missing my old friend. It had been a couple years since I had seen him. I barely missed him a few months earlier at the Fort Worth Stock Show.

"What I would give to see Bobby," I thought to myself. Little did I know, Bobby would come see me three weeks later.

By that time it was getting a little warm outside. After all it was the first part of May. I loaded another bag of books and decided to work the stands where it was cool. I do pretty good working the stands, that's where all the wives are. You see it might be fun to watch your husband but anyone else is like watching paint dry. A good book is just what Dr. Bill ordered.

I was halfway through my second bag of books when I saw a young mother carrying her disabled son. It took me back decades. My mother must have looked like her when she carried me before I could walk. To say it touched me would be an understatement.

17

I have run into parents before with a disabled child and I always try to talk to them. Now I don't see myself as special. Who I am today is because of my mother and the good Lord. Seeing what I have done with my life, or what God has done with my life, perhaps offers hope.

So like I have done before, I went and sat down with the boy and his mother. Before long she asked me what all of the people ask me. "How did you get so independent?"

The answer is an easy one but it tends to leave parents confused. "My mother allowed and actually pushed me to be independent," I told the young mother.

I saw my opening when she asked me to explain. I put it in this book because I feel it is important. The easiest thing to do when you have a special-needs child is to be overprotective. Though it may be easy, as well as natural, it doesn't mean it is right.

I use myself as an example. There was me and in the next town was a girl like me. While my mother let me run and have my fun, this girl's parents never let her out of their sight. I learned to drive; her folks took her everywhere. I went to college; she stayed at her house. I saw the real world; she saw what her folks allowed her to see.

The sad part is when her folks were gone she had none of the skills she needed to live independently. With no one there, she was forced into a nursing home, far before her time. To me over protection of a special-needs child is a form of child abuse.

I then told her my mother didn't put limitations on me. She allowed me to find my own limitations. Her only rule was, "Don't come home crying if you get hurt; learn from it and move on. My mother's words sometimes came back to bite her in the backside, like the time I came home with a motorcycle. I know she really had to bite her tongue that day.

The young mother was in tears when I had finished my little speech. At first I felt bad. I didn't mean to make her cry. But she assured me that they were good tears. She said she had learned more from me in fifteen minutes than she had learned from most of the doctors she had spoken with. I told her it wasn't me at all but my dear departed mother and the Lord speaking through me.

She hugged me and I gave her my number. It dawned on me that my job was more than writing and selling books. In the weeks that followed that became more apparent. I walked away with a single thought.

"My mother could not save me from myself, but she gave me the armor to take on the world."

Later on that afternoon I met the young mother's husband. He seemed like a real nice guy but almost like his wife, he didn't have a clue. But who does with their first child, let alone a special-needs child? I could tell he was doing his best and that's all anyone has a right to ask. I am very sure my mother didn't have all the answers either.

Before I knew it, it was nearly 7 o'clock, and I was getting hungry. I had a good day so why not call it a day. I found my trusted mount a place for the evening and I was out of there. Mexican food was all I had on my mind.

I knew from all the times I had driven through town, just where to go. It just happened to be across from my motel. When I drove into the parking lot, there wasn't a car one. I thought the place was closed. But I was craving Mexican food so I tried the door. I was in luck. The place was open.

A couple came in after I had placed my order. I didn't pay them no mind and I thought they didn't me either. I was just so hungry that the roof could have been caving in and I would not have noticed. Needless to say, my meal was consumed in nothing flat.

I was just fixing to pay out when the man came up to me.

"Aren't you the guy that writes the cowboy books?" he asked. I told him I was and reached out to shake his hand.

"You don't happen to have any of your books with you?" was his second question.

I told him they were out in the truck and if he had a minute, I'd go get him one. He smiled a big smile and I was out to get the man my latest novel.

So all in all, my second day at the roping was great. I got to talk to my old Billy and I made a new friend who knew my dear friend Bobby Deane. Through my experiences growing up with a disability, I offered two young parents hope with their own special-needs child. Then to top it off, someone stopped me at supper wanting a book. My day had been blessed. It would have been blessed even if I didn't sell a single book, so it was richly blessed.

One more day and I would be headed home. Home with my pockets flush, new memories made and a good feeling.

CHAPTER 2

INTO THE DARKNESS

My third day at the roping consisted of selling a few more books and tying up a few loose ends. By noon I was ready to call it a show. I figured if I left, I would avoid the roper's version of a traffic jam. In two hours I'd be home. Let me tell you, I figured that all wrong. It didn't take a couple of hours for me to get home, it took two months.

I left out of there feeling good about my weekend's work. Life was good and I had made a few more friends. I was sure to thank the Lord as I did some more windshield time. I was looking forward to seeing my critters at home.

When I hit Hico, I was getting hungry. There is a T in the road in this small town. If I turned left, I would go to Stephenville. If I did that I would avoid the traffic in Weatherford. But if I went right, I could stop at Hammons for a little barbeque. I was starving so I turned right. If only I knew what awaited my fate, I would have taken the left.

If you want some good Texas barbeque and want to meet some really good people, you can't beat Hammons or the Ranch house in Glen Rose for both. I have been eating there for years. Whatever fate awaited me, at least it would find me with a full belly.

I had a full stomach and a smile when I found myself on the move again.

I cannot say I remember a whole lot after making the turn toward Weatherford. I remember hearing this chopping sound, the sound like at the beginning of the old TV show M.A.S.H. That was right before everything went black.

Somehow I was transported through time and space. My landing spot was at Will Rogers in the John Justin Arena. I looked around and not another human being could be seen. My Hoveround had been replaced by an old-time wheelchair - the kind from the nineteenth century with the big wheels in the front.

I was really starting to get confused. Why would I be at Will Rogers if there were no people? Why would I come without books to sell? No people, no books - it was then I realized something was wrong. Later I figured out this is when I knew I was hurt. The wheelchair was a dead giveaway.

About this time my white Town Car pulled up and I climbed in the back. Later I would wonder if Rod Steiger from the old TV show **The Twilight Zone** was driving. I was sure I was somewhere other than where I was headed when I left Hamilton. Was I dead? I didn't know because I had never been dead before. It's kind of like you only do it once.

My next question was, "Where is my Town Car taking me and what happened to my SUV?" Then the car stopped at a welcome sight. It was the home of my adopted family, Susan and Ty.

"I can't be dead," I told myself when I saw Susan and Ty. "This must be the mother of all nightmares," I thought to myself.

Susan came running out to me when she saw I was hurt and Ty was right behind her.

"I don't know what to do, I don't think I can go home." It was my voice saying the words.

"What about your dogs?" she asked. "My dogs, my dogs; what about me?" I asked.

"I know where to go, you are going to be alright," Susan said in a soft voice, right before everything went black again.

The next time I woke up I was in a hospital bed. I had all kinds of tubes running in and out of my body. I was in no hospital room. I was in a horse stall in a barn. I knew where I was. I was on the Double J Ranch in one of John and JJ's horse stalls, but why?

From my makeshift ICU room, I could see everything happening in the arena. There was my best friend Susan working with an equine flag. I marveled at her awhile, for she has always had patience with kids and horses.

"John and JJ must have given her a job while I recovered," I said in my head.

Then the event turned to roping. I saw the funniest thing I ever saw at a roping. These two team ropers were wearing slacks and neckties. Just when I thought it couldn't get any stranger, these two duded-up ropers appeared in my hospital room horse stall. Come to find out, they were my doctors. One of them said his name was Dr. Rush. I never did catch the other's name.

The next morning got even stranger. Here came my old buddy Zach Terry rolling another hospital bed into the stall next to me.

"JJ said you needed some company, so I picked Rick up at the Sherman Hospital. He is waiting for a lung transplant. We have two more coming in tonight," my old college buddy informed me. Rick was JJ's dad.

"What in the world is going on? Has the whole world lost its ever-loving mind?" I asked myself.

What I didn't know was I was in some kind of alternative universe. It couldn't have been a dream; dreams didn't last that long. I couldn't have been dead because everyone around me was alive. About that time I felt a hand touch mine. I looked to see who it was and it was Susan. She was wearing a yellow-and-black checkered shirt. I could see it clear as day.

"Don't worry Wild Bill, everything is going to be alright," she said.

Something was up. In all the years I had known her, she had never called me Wild Bill. That was the handle Bob Kurtz had hung around my neck.

The doctor came in about that time and gave me something to rest. Visions of Susan and her yellow-and-black shirt faded from sight. I slept off into an actual dream, not the trip I was on.

In my dream, I was a little boy again. I stood in front of Sunny Boy, my very first horse. I petted the colt's nose and wondered if I would ever be able to ride him. I must have been about 5 years of age in the dream. I know this because I was wearing the braces I wore when I was 5. In the background I could hear my mother calling me, "Billy Joe, Billy Joe," as she always called me. Then I was awake again - or was I.

This time I had slipped the surly bonds on my horse stall. I was back in the nineteenth century wheelchair. There was a loud sound of a public announcer system ringing in my ears. I could not make out what was being said at first.

"Come join us, come join us at the Tyson Chicken Church. Come watch us ordain our new high priest," is what it sounded like.

If being in a horse-stall hospital room and cared for by a couple of team doctors was strange, this was getting plum weird. Especially when I looked down to find my toenails had been painted. Alice did not go down the rabbit hole, I did.

There was a long line of people waiting outside an office door. I knew these people, they were all the vendors at the horse shows I had once gone to. Jon Conklin was the last in line. I thought I'd see what everyone was waiting in line for.

"Hey Jon, what is everyone waiting for?" I asked my old friend.

"Brother Bill, you didn't hear? Man this Tyson Chicken Church is the hottest thing going. If you get you a vending spot, you'll have it made," he said while not answering my question or noticing the wheelchair I was in.

"But who are you waiting to see," I asked again.

"Jon and JJ Carpenter, didn't you hear. They are in charge now. Jon will be the new high priest of the Tyson Church," he responded.

"It sounds more like a cult to me," I told him.

"You need to go inside and check it out, man," was his advice to me.

"Why not?" Why not go have a look-see behind the privacy fence," I told myself. And so I did.

I wheeled myself in through the gate. Inside there was a carnival-like atmosphere. There were jugglers, sword swallowers and the whole circus nine yards. And just when I thought I was in someone's acid trip, it became ghostly quiet. After a short silence, horns began to sound off as my attention was directed toward a stage.

Dark-skinned men with their bodies painted with some sort of white clay took the stage. The crowd of people grew silent. Native drums began a monotone sound as the painted men began to dance a strange, chicken-like dance. The loud speaker I had heard earlier was even louder.

"Join us, join us and join the people born from the egg. Celebrate with us and welcome our new high priest. We give you the Carpenter's," the voice announced. Then on a big screen behind the stage, I saw my friend Jon Carpenter.

People in the audience began to throw chicken parts. I didn't know if I was at a cult revival or an Alice Cooper concert. At any rate, I was wishing I was back in the horse stall.

I guess someone heard my cries because the next thing I knew I was back outside the fence. The line waiting to get into the office was longer than ever. I couldn't believe what my eyes were seeing. There at the back of the line was Susan's mother and brother, Lonnie.

"Just what in the name of the Almighty are they doing here?" I asked myself, all dazed and confused. I knew Lonnie was no vendor and with this nutty atmosphere, whatever it is, it is no place for mom, (that's what I have always called Susan's mother).

"Lonnie, what are you two doing here," I asked Susan's brother.

"Mom's friend wants to be a vendor, so Mom wanted to see what it was all about. Bill, I tell you it's all over the radio," he responded.

"It ought to be. Every fruitcake known to the free world is here," I thought to myself.

"Lonnie you need to get mom out of here before she gets hit with a chicken neck or leg. I tell you Lonnie, they're slinging chicken parts like baseballs. This in no place for any of us," I said as he looked at me like I had lost my mind.

Hell, I did lose my mind. I saw hospital beds in horse stalls, team-roping doctors and now this: an amusement park for chicken lovers. I had gone around the bend more than once.

And just when I heard it all, there came a familiar voice, "Shine 'em up." I didn't need to look to know who it was but I did anyway. Over by the entrance was Red's and Norman's shoeshine stand, just like at the Fort Worth Stock Show.

It was all too much, even for me, the fiction writer. I was beginning to feel like I had gotten lost in Stephen King's thought process. I had to find a place to take all the insanity in because I knew I was fixing to lose it.

I saw a park bench in the distance and on the park bench sat a beautiful blonde-haired lady. It looked as though she was at peace. I thought perhaps she wouldn't mind sharing a little with me. I could use a little peace.

The closer I got to the woman, the more she looked like Sherri, a lady I always thought as my older sister. Her late husband was one of the best friends I ever had.

"Oh my Lord, it is Sherri," I said as she smiled at me. A sense of relief seemed to rush through me as I reached out for her hand.

The we were both transported back to my horse stall in Jon and JJ's barn. I didn't care; it beat the hell out of the chicken cult. I held on to Sherri's hand like I never wanted to let go.

They tell me this is when I woke up but it seemed like I was still in my alternative universe, still in my horse stall. Sherri told me the doctor came in and said, "It looks like somebody finally woke up."

But that's not what I heard. What I heard was, "I get off in an hour, we can go out to dinner then." This want-to-be team roper was hitting on my big sister.

"Bill you have been in a coma," Sherri informed me.

"No Sherri I've been in a barn, I'm still in a barn. You need to get me to a real hospital," I pleaded.

"No Bill, you were in a car wreck. You've been in a coma, and you are in the hospital in Fort Worth," she tried her best to explain.

I could still smell the sawdust shavings in my stall. I could still see the arena down below. I should know where I was so drug-induced Bill was having none of it.

"Sherri just get me out of this stall and take me to the Decatur hospital. They know me there," I once again pleaded.

Sherri could see I wasn't quite ready to leave my alternative universe, so she went along with the gag; kind of like a straight person does with a comic.

"All right, whatever you say Bill," said Sherri trying her best to comfort me.

She had no sooner spoke those words when I thought my salvation came through the gate of my stall. It was Susan's son, Brandon. Now despite all the rumors circling around, I never had children of my own, but I have always thought of Brandon and his sister, Tyla, as the closest thing I would ever have to kids of my own. I thank Ty and Susan for sharing them with me.

Like me, Brandon was an educated man. Surely he could see where I was and where I needed to be.

"Sherri, could I have a minute with Brandon?" I asked of my dear friend.

"I'll go get me some coffee while you to talk," or at least that is what I think she said. Come to think of it, I have never seen Sherri have a cup of coffee, unlike myself who nearly mainlines it. I bet Brandon wishes she would have given him a heads-up on my nutty state of mind.

I waited until this sweet woman left the room before I started pleading my case with the one I was sure would understand.

"Brandon," I whispered. "You have to get me out of this barn. You have to get me to a real hospital," I told him.

If you have never met me before, let me tell you that I am not the easiest person in the world to understand. Now if you add all the drugs they had running through my body, not to mention that I wasn't making a lick of sense, you might understand the confused look on Brandon's face.

"What!" was about all could get out of him.

Seeing his confusion, I tried to speak in the clearest voice I had. Never mind, I wasn't making any sense.

"I don't know why but someone has put me in a barn. If I am as bad as Sherri says I am, I need a real hospital," I said, trying my best to explain to the young man.

"You are in a real hospital, Bill." Brandon said the same thing as Sherri had said but it still didn't sink in.

"Brandon, just help me to the elevator and let's go find a hospital," I said once more.

"Bill, you are a smart man. If you were in a barn, how could there be an elevator?" was the question my dear Brandon posed.

"Because Jon and JJ have money. They can have anything they want in their barn," was my answer to his question. But I am not so sure I answered him out loud. It might have been in my head.

It was about that time when Sherri stuck her head in the door. "Can I come back in now?" she asked.

She must have been a welcome sight for Brandon. Later she told me she had asked Brandon what we talked about. She said he couldn't answer because he had no idea.

It must have been later on that day, or maybe the next day, when I finally realized I was in a real hospital. It doesn't mean I wasn't still seeing things that were not there.

I think it was later on that evening when I saw this Mexican women come through the door. She walked halfway across the room before getting down on her hands and knees. I watched as she crawled under my hospital bed and began poking me.

Frantically I pushed the button to the nurse stationed right outside my door. Just imagine the look on her face when I told her there was a girl under my bed poking me. She told me there was no one under my bed. I then asked to see the doctor because she didn't believe me.

Enters Dr. Rush, the same team roper from my coma. It was the same man who had been hitting on Sherri earlier - or so I thought. None of that seemed to matter. There was a girl under my bed poking me.

"The nurse says you have some sort of problem, Mr. Chambers," Dr. Rush stated in a professional voice.

"You might say that. A Mexican girl came in about twenty minutes ago and crawled under my bed. I can feel her tugging at me and poking me," I informed the good doctor.

"Now Mr. Chambers, why would there be someone under you bed?" he wanted to know.

"Hell, I don't know, maybe she's out for the copper wire. All I know is she is under the bed. Humor me, just look," I exclaimed.

To his credit, he did look under the bed. What happened next I'll never forget.

"Bill, you are just stoned. Go with it, son." Those were probably the funniest words the man ever spoke. I still laugh when I think about it.

The next morning when I woke up I was still in a drug-induced haze. I really didn't know what world I was going to wake up in. I didn't know if I was going to wake up in a barn, a hospital or where. I was halfway afraid to look around.

I did have myself a good look around as soon as could focus. My friend Jon Carpenter was the first thing a saw. Jon is a pretty big guy, kind of hard to miss.

Later I was told he had spent every night with me when I was in my coma. That may be the definition of the word "friend." Either that or he thought he was in the will. No folks, I was just kidding, Jon is as good as they come.

"Jon, am I a quadriplegic?" were the first words out of my mouth.

"No, but you still have cerebral palsy," he actually said with a straight face, right before he started laughing. I muttered some obscenity in his direction and went back to sleep.

I do not know why I remember everything that happened so vividly, but if the truth be told, the next few weeks are a blur. Perhaps it is the writer in me who loves a good story. My mother always said I had a good imagination. It was not always a good thing in her eyes. I often tell people that I make my living doing what my mother used to whip my butt for - telling stories.

I have spent weeks trying to figure out the meaning of all my far-out adventures during those four days I spent in a coma - from my hospital stall in Jon and JJ's barn to the chicken cult. There has to be some meaning somewhere in the madness. Like why were my toenails painted, why did my best friend seem more concerned with my critters having food to eat or why was I alone at Will Rogers?

You see, believe it or not, I am a man of reason. In my way of seeing the world, anything and everything can be explained. It took a long time to put the pieces to my abstract puzzle together. In the next chapter I would like to share my findings with you.

CHAPTER 3

MEANWHILE BACK ON THE RANCH

In the first part of this chapter, I will clue you all in on what was going on in the real world while I was in my horse stall in la-la land. This will be a tick-tock account of the happenings: from the car wreck up to the point where I ended the last chapter.

In the second half of the chapter, I will tell you the meaning I have found when I was in my alternative universe. For both sections of this part of the book, I had to depend on the memory of my friends, doctors and police reports. That was more so for the first half than the second.

The last thing I remember was turning south on State Highway 144 just outside of Glen Rose. According to Officer Hill's report, a car headed north drifted past the centerline and hit me head on. My SUV rolled several times before coming to rest in the bar ditch.

According to Hill's report, the two young men in the car said the one driving went to sleep. This is all the information I could obtain from the trooper's report.

I learned more about my wreck from the witnesses who saw it unfold before their eyes. My SUV rolled but that was only half of the story. I came out of the passenger's window on the first roll and the vehicle then rolled over the top of me. As a result my chest was crushed.

What the officer's report failed to mention was these two boys had ran more than one car off the road before they got to me. They just didn't doze off. Their erratic driving had been going on for miles. A victim of their sleeping while driving already had 911 on the phone before they hit me. I do not understand why the accounts of these witnesses were not anywhere on the police report.

There are a lot of things missing from the report I received. A statement from the onlookers who were playing golf that day would have been nice. You see the place where the crash occurred on Highway 144 borders the local golf course. Some even jumped the fence to help out.

There are other statements missing as well. The Game Warden was the first on the scene. Where is his statement and what about the first trooper to arrive? There are a lot of questions I would like to ask him - like why wasn't a field sobriety test given to the driver of the car that hit me?

There is one more question I would like to ask the trooper. There he was at a major automobile accident and he didn't run the "proof of insurance" card he was given. That would come back to haunt me weeks later when we found out the card was bogus. You see for weeks, my lawyer, I and everyone else involved thought there would be a settlement.

I guess I could talk all day about what should have happened that didn't. But I won't. All I can do is tell you, the reader, what happened next according to the people who were there.

A very nice lady, who later came to see me in the hospital, said she sat with me until help arrived. Later I would find out her husband came and sat with me the first couple of nights I was in the hospital. To me, that kind of makes up for all the things that were not done. You see there are a lot of good people in the world. These were just the first two I would meet on my journey back.

I have said the last thing I remember was a chopping sound, like the sound of the beginning of the TV show "M.A.S.H." I believe the sound was coming from the Care Flight helicopter that was sent for me.

It was days later that I learned about my first helicopter ride and, wouldn't you know it, I don't remember it at all. I know I rode it though because I have the $32,000 bill to prove it. Yes, $32,000 for 45 minutes. Friends, we are in the wrong business.

Somewhere along the way, I did the one thing no cowboy wants to admit. I lost my cowboy boots. To this day no one knows what happened to them or my brand-new, store-bought teeth. It's a mystery I might just write my next book on.

The next stop on this wild ride was at Harris Hospital in downtown Fort Worth. Harris is a Methodist Hospital. I was raised Methodist, so if it was here I was to make my final stand, it seemed fitting.

The list of my injuries was pretty long to say the least. Because I was crushed, all my ribs on the left side were busted. My lungs had been punctured by one of my broken ribs, my heart was out of place, my spleen ruptured and my pelvis was fractured in more than one place.

If you didn't know me better, you would think I was one of those crazy-ass bull riders - and not a very good one. I would like to say I have better sense, but everyone knows that isn't so.

Do you know what amazes me to this day? With all these injuries, there was not a mark on my body anywhere. It is almost like the Good Lord looked down and said, "This boy is ugly enough."

My friends, those are the nuts and bolts of all that happened to me that day, May 3, 2015. There is not a single part of it that I remember. I tell folks that everyone knew of my wreck before I did.

The character Joseph in the Old Testament of the Bible had the power to find meaning in the dreams of others. He was sold into slavery for that very reason. Years later, the gift would get him out of prison. I guess it is all in the timing.

I have always thought dreams held meaning although I never have tried to figure what someone else's dream may or may not mean. I have looked at my own and some way, I have found their meaning.

My mother has been gone since 1992. From time to time, I dream about her. I figure it is only in my dreams that she can visit me. The same thing goes for Bob Kurtz. The only thing is I don't remember Bob working as hard as he does in my dreams.

Webster defines the word "coma" as a state of prolonged unconsciousness. I think a better way to define it is "a prolonged state of sleep." Maybe I am just splitting hairs but I have been knocked unconscious before and I do not remember dreaming. When I was in my coma, I was in a state of dreaming.

My dreams were so vivid I couldn't help but want to find their meaning right down to the painted toenails. After five days of being in this state, wouldn't anyone wonder what God or your mind is trying to tell you?

In the first part on my dream, I was alone at Will Rogers in the John Justin Arena. It was confusing at first. Then I learned there was no way for them to contact anyone who knew me. I was still using my Arizona driver license and my cell phone had been lost at the scene. With the exception of the lady's husband who sat with me, I was alone, maybe the most alone I had ever been.

I wasn't there in my Hoveround, I was in a wheelchair. I have fought all my life to stay out of a wheelchair and there I was. What it told me was I was hurt, and hurt bad.

The next question was how did I get hurt? My answer came in the form of my white Town Car. It is true that I owned the car but I didn't drive it that often. The last vehicle I remembered driving was my SUV. I added up everything and it screamed automobile accident.

The previous winter I had fallen on the ice and knocked my front teeth out. Susan's husband, Ty, was the one who put in the call to 911 that time. Someone had the idea to see if I had a history with the emergency number. Sure enough, they found the call Ty had made months earlier. A few moments after someone called Ty at work, my Town Car was pulling into his drive and I was no longer alone in my coma.

This is where Susan took control both in my dream state and in the real world. The first thing she did was to review my phone bill. Susan then began calling the numbers I called the most. In turn it would lead to the number of Jon and JJ on the Double J Ranch. I guess Susan knew it would be better if they took the lead.

I guess this is when I went to the Double J Ranch in my coma. I still haven't figured out why I thought I was in a horse stall in a barn. Perhaps I never will. I tend to chalk it up to the over-active imagination of a writer.

I have yet to explain certain details of this part of the coma-induced dream, like my team-roping doctors. I know why I thought they were ropers. After all I had just left a roping before the wreck. What I can't figure out is why Dr. Rush looked the same in real life as he did in my dream.

In the previous chapter, I spoke of a yellow-and-black checkered shirt that Susan had worn in the arena and when she came up to see me in my stall. Come to find out, it is the very shirt she wore when she came to the hospital to see me.

How did I know what Dr. Rush looked like? How did I know what shirt Susan had on when she came to visit me? How did I know these things when my eyes were closed? I really don't have a logical explanation but I do have a theory.

They say when a person is in a coma, they can still hear things around them. That part is true. That is how I ended up with painted toenails. When my friend Shelly came to see me in ICU, she threatened to paint my toenails if I didn't wake up. The next thing I know is they were painted in my alternative universe. I guess I didn't wake up.

What if we have some kind of sixth sense when we are in a coma? What if we have a limited sight in this state? It would explain how I knew what Dr. Rush looked like when I woke up and what Susan was wearing when she came to see me. I knew it just like I knew what Shelly said to me.

Here is a little scary insight from the beyond. Remember in my last chapter, I said the doctor came in and gave me something to sleep? I then began to dream, a dream in a dream, if you will.

In this dream I was a little boy again, wearing the braces I wore as a child. I was standing in front of my horse Sunny Boy and petting him. In the distance I could hear my mother calling my name.

Later on Susan told me my heart had stopped beating at least twice. I was the closest to death's door than I have ever been. I didn't see a bright light at the end of a tunnel like has been described in other near-death experiences but to me my mother's voice calling me was close enough.

The second time they lost my heartbeat, I not only heard my mother's voice but I actually had a conversation with her. I think I was ready to cross over but she told me I wasn't finished yet and that I had to go back.

I did not remember this part of my coma/dream. Sherri said I told her all about it when I first came out of the fog. Now I don't know why I was given a second chance but I hope whatever it is, I make my momma proud.

A small note from the writer: I never did ride Sunny Boy but I have ridden lots of other horses in my life. I have competed in numerous World Shows and last year I even took Reserve World Champion in Western pleasure. What I would have given to had been aboard Sunny Boy that day.

The next morning, when I saw my college buddy Zach rolling in and JJ's dad putting him in the stall next to me, it had a bit of meaning to it. Jon had gotten hold of my college buddy and told him about the wreck. He and Rick, JJ's dad, had come to see me. Rick is on an oxygen bottle. I guess I dreamed what I did because they were there one after another.

Now for the craziest portion of my dream: the chicken cult. I would like to say it was a bad acid trip, but it wasn't. Yes, I spent my misguided youth in the '70s but I never tripped.

This is how I have this part of my five-day dream figured: JJ is part of the Tyson family, as in Tyson Chicken. Don Tyson, the founder of this multi-billion-dollar corporation, had died a few years earlier. All accounts say Don was a colorful man who loved beautiful woman. That would explain Ramona, a looker if I ever saw one. You might say Don Tyson was a man after my own heart.

It was about this time in my coma, that they had found my long-lost sister, Katy Sue. She was living not too far from where Jon had grown up in Arkansas. My sister has MS and that makes it hard for her to travel. And so it was decided, I guess by all those involved, that Jon would take over and make the decisions that I couldn't while I was in my coma state.

I think in my coma, I equated taking over my care to taking over the chicken fortune. Me being nearly as colorful as Don, I took it a step too far. I guess that is how a major corporation built on yard bird was twisted into chicken cult. You can blame that on one crazy-ass writer in a coma and that is how Jon Carpenter became the high priest in this cult, if only for a moment.

Regarding the horse shows Jon and I go to, I forgot to mention that when Jon isn't a high priest in my coma, in the real world he is a horse trainer - and a pretty good one. Well, as I was saying, the horse shows we go to are nearly like a traveling circus. In a traveling circus you have people who make up the core of the circus. In the horse world we call then vendors.

Do you remember from the last chapter, the long line of people waiting to see Jon and JJ? Those were the vendors we see at almost every horse show. Hell what am I saying? When you get down to it, I am a vendor.

About all I can say is, "Thank the good Lord that Sherri was there to help pull me out of one crazy dream. It could have gotten a lot stranger if she didn't take my hand when she did."

Some of you have read most all my books. If so, you might recognize the names in an author's tale of being in a coma. Nearly every one of these names has appeared in one of my books. In retrospect, can I be real sure who was in my coma? Was it my dear friends or the characters I created in my books? I would like to think it was a little of both - just because my friends are not that weird. But who's to say?

So what meaning did I get from my time in a coma? That is the question you might ask. The first would be that I am loved and that I would be missed. The second is God must have something in mind for me to do. There is no way I should be here writing this book. The last thing I got out of being in a coma for days is, "It is going to take more than a little fender bender to kill my vivid imagination."

CHAPTER 4

BACK AMONG THE LIVING

I don't remember very much those first few days after coming out of my coma. I do however remember the first question Dr. Rush asked me. "Mr. Chambers, just how many brothers and sisters do you have?"

I can only guess that the good doctor could see the confused look I had on my face. More than likely he had to ask himself if it was the question or the drugs.

"You see we have a rule about giving out information about our patients. We can only give out such information to the immediate family. I bet we have had a hundred different people call in from all over the county claiming to be a brother or a sister," Dr. Rush informed me.

I just shrugged my shoulders but inside I felt like saying, "Well Doc the old man got around," was my unvoiced thought.

The same rule also applied to visitors but my posse blew that rule out of the water from the get go. I guess the nurses just finally gave up asking what relation the person was to me. I do not remember ever being alone the rest of the time I was in ICU. It seemed like every time I woke up there was someone new sitting in the chair by my bed.

I would wake up and there would be Gordon. Then the next time I opened my eyes, there was Richard Mercer. You might ask yourself if I was dreaming, after all I was heavily medicated. But no I wasn't dreaming. I have the memory of the dirty looks the nurses gave me to prove it.

Ss soon as my thoughts cleared a little, I wondered how all of these folk knew I had been in a wreck. A few days earlier no one knew where I was. I talk to Susan at least once a day; that is my M.O. She said at first she wasn't overly concerned because I told her I might go across the river and do a little gambling. By the third day, she said she was getting worried.

It seems to me after the fifth day, everyone I had ever known just where I was. I might be an educated man but that doesn't mean I am high tech. The only reason I have a computer is to write my novels. I have no need of the Internet and all the things people get lost in. Believe it or not, I still have a flip phone. You might say I don't do change well.

What I am getting at is, I know very little about this thing called Facebook. The only thing I knew about Facebook was I wished I had invented it. That Mark guy is a gazillionaire by now. Anyway this Facebook thing must be better than CNN.

Jon and JJ set me up a Facebook page while I was visiting la-la land, Never Ever Land and the great Here Ever After. Later on, when I was of sound mind, they would take turns reading the well wishes to me. Somehow it helped me want to get better. I never dreamed that I or my writing could have touched so many folks.

The job of handling my Facebook page has now fallen to Sherri. I asked her how she does it and she said, "I act like I am you." I had to ask if that meant she talked funny as well. If you know me, you know I have an off-the-wall sense of humor.

Nancy, who you will meet later in the chapter, called me the other day and asked who I had running my Facebook page.

"I know it isn't you because you cannot type that fast or spell that good," she said. We both had a good laugh.

Anyway, where was I, I regress. As I was saying, I've never seen nothing like it. Facebook had let the whole world know I was down but not out. People I hadn't heard from in thirty years were sending best wishes to me. I think I might have been the only one not on Facebook. But I guess, I can't say that anymore - well kind of.

The story about my wreck wasn't only on Facebook. Glory Ann Kurtz shared with all her readers both about the automobile accident as well as my recovery. The cards, checks and letters from my family in the cutting world are a direct result of her blog **AllAboutCutting.com**, as well as her caring for me. She was one of the few who were there when my writing career started and she has helped me all along the way.

I have also been told that ***Quarter Horse News*** also ran a story about me. I have yet to read it but I look forward to it. It was this publication and Glory Ann that put this traveling writer and cowboy poet on the map many years ago. And so I thank them for the years of support.

Meanwhile, back in the ICU unit, I was learning what it was like to be lost in the desert without water. My favorite word became "ice chip." Because the doctors had to inflate my lungs, they were worried about my water intake. When I tried to drink water, I began to choke. What they didn't know, and we tried to tell them, was I always choke a little. Needless to say, they thought I still might take some water into my lungs and I guess that was a bad thing.

I could have ice chips even though I wasn't allowed any water. The deal was I could only have one ice chip at a time. It was nearly enough to drive me mad. I have never been so thirsty in my life. If I wasn't completely mad, I was sure driving everyone around me mad.

I do not care if it was Jon, Sherri or anyone who came into the room, I begged for an ice chip. I mean I really begged, like a dog I begged. If a person was just walking down the hall, I would yell, "Hey, would you give me an ice chip?" I am dead serious. But I wouldn't act like that when Susan was around. I always behaved myself. No wonder everyone liked it when she came to visit.

One time someone gave me an ice chip, then made the mistake of leaving it within my reach. Just imagine a starving dog and an unattended T-bone. You get the idea. I was all over it. It was well worth the scolding I took from Jon.

You think I was happy when I got my first drink of water? Just think how happy everyone around me was. A thirsty Wild Bill was not the best of patients, to say the least.

Earlier I told how my cell phone had been lost at the location of the accident. It was one of the reasons the hospital couldn't find anyone who knew me. I was declared a John Doe so they could perform emergency surgery. It is more than likely what saved my life.

Well, one day Sherri came to see me and low and behold, there sat my phone right next to the bed.

"Bill, is that your phone?" she asked thinking like everyone else that it was lost.

"Yep, it showed up some time last night while I was asleep. I'll tell you one thing Sis. There are some spooky things happening around here. Just the other night this little Mexican girl climbed under my bed and started poking me," I informed her.

"I know Bill, you tell me that story every time I come to see you," Sherri said to me.

"I did? My short-term memory seems to have been banged up like the rest of my body. There isn't anything working right anymore," I confessed.

"It still doesn't explain how your phone just appeared out of thin air," Sherri pointed out.

"Don't ask me, I am still trying to figure out what happened to that little Mexican girl under my bed," I said, halfway joking.

The real answer behind my phone showing up in my room goes something like this. The day before Susan and Ty had gone to see my totaled-out

Expedition, they wanted to see if there was anything left worth saving and take some pictures of the best vehicle I ever owned. Old Red was headed for the scrap heap for sure.

Susan looked under my driver's seat and low and behold there was my phone. You would think as many people that were around the day of the wreck that someone would have the good sense to look under the seat. That reminds me to ask her if she saw my boots or my store-bought teeth while she was under there.

That night she had given me my cell phone when she came to visit. I was so doped up that I didn't remember it. So there you have it, the case of the re-appearing cell phone solved.

I cannot say which one of us came up with idea to start calling people from my call list. It sounds more like one of my hair-brained ideas than it does Sherri's. In my way of thinking there were a few, maybe not many, who hadn't heard what a fix I was in.

The calls got briefly delayed because Sherri and I had a bit of a spat over which button to push on my flip phone. You know how these folks are with a smart phone. They think they know everything.

"Who do you want to call first?" Sherri asked after I let her have her way. You cannot tell me we don't sound like brother and sister, right down to the little arguments over nothing. Most of the time we act like the middle-age adults we are, but not always and not that day. At least I was no longer trying to convince her I was in a barn.

One name came to mind. And I was certain he hadn't heard the news because I knew he was tied up at Valley Ranch. Wade Wilson is the quarterback coach for the Dallas Cowboys. He is also one of the reasons I didn't die a drunk.

I met Wade some 36 years ago at East Texas State University. He was the star quarterback and I was a freshman. In the spring we played on the same softball team. To say Wade was my friend would not do him justice. Wade was my hero.

Wade was drafted by the Minnesota Vikings that year. The legend of Wade Wilson grew and I became a drunk. Many years later, when I was at the end of my rope, the Vikings were playing a Sunday game. As in college, I never missed a chance to watch my old friend play.

Something was a little different that day. I began to wonder what he would think if he could see what I had become. My hero from college would not be proud of the man I had become. And just like the old days when he lead the Lions down to score, thoughts of my quarterback lead me out of the darkness of my drunkenness. I have not had a drink since that Sunday in 1987.

Wade and I reconnected some years back and I even honored him by putting him in my book, "***One Ranger's Justice***." I guess now he is in another one.

Now you know why I wanted to call my old quarterback first. I was all right and he had been working and hadn't heard about the wreck. I assured him that I would be all right and it would take more than a couple joy-riding kids to kill me. He laughed but still I could hear the concern in his voice.

Later on he and Tony Romo sent me a couple of autographed footballs. I gave one to the Challenge Riders and they auctioned it off to support their cause. The second ball I will raffle off in the fall. You might ask what I got out of it. Well this season, I went to my first NFL game as Wade's guest.

I don't know who else we called after getting off the phone with Wade. You might say my meds kicked in. There was a lot of that during those early days. I could be talking to someone and doze off in the middle of a conversation.

I think it was the last day I was in ICU when Bruce and Nancy came all the way from West Texas to see me. You would think they have to have Facebook out there because they sure don't have any trees. I know because that is where I am from. I have often told people, I was 18 before I saw my first tree.

I have known Nancy most of my life. We lived across the street from her folks, and her daddy was the preacher at the church we went to. I use to run with Nancy's little brother and she was already married with kids by the time we got to high school.

Nancy's little brother was the typical preacher's son, into everything, and I was usually with him. He and I had the same ritual ever Sunday morning - one of us would have to get the other out of trouble. We would have to go find my pickup because every Sunday it was missing. Then we would go to church. That was just one of the joys of growing up in a small town in the '70s.

Nancy's family sort of adopted me after my mother died. Every Christmas, wedding or graduation, no matter what, I was invited. To this day, every time I go to Abilene, Nancy, Bruce and I will go out to dinner.

I do not know why it was such a surprise to see them, but it was. We spent most of that afternoon talking about the old days and the trouble her little brother and I would often find ourselves in. At one point we even called Ole Blondie. You see where I am from everyone had a nickname.

It was almost like I wasn't in a bad wreck while we talked on the phone. We yelled the same insults at each other, just like old times. That's one thing I learned out of all of this, it's hard to beat family and friends.

I would like to end this chapter with a funny story; a story relayed to me just the other night by Sherri. Believe it or not, Sherri was at another hospital in Oklahoma when she got the call about the two-car pileup on highway 144. She was there waiting for her granddaughter to be born. It was like one was trying to check in and one was trying to trying to check out.

Like I wrote earlier, there was a time when the hospital didn't know who to contact or anything about me. All they knew was that they had a man whose SUV landed on him and he was in mighty bad shape. In fact, so bad the doctors had many operations in mind for him.

Sherri's grandbaby was born then she high tailed it back to Texas to see about me. She said she hadn't been in my room long when Dr. Rush came in.

"Are you family?" he asked

"Yes, I am his sister," Sherri says she answered.

"So you are Katy Sue. I have been trying to reach you all day," the good doctor explained.

"No, I am Sherri. I am not his blood sister; we just tell everyone we are brother and sister.

"I should run you out, but if you can tell me a little more about Mr. Chambers, I'll let you stay. You see Mr. Chambers is in really bad shape," said Dr. Rush. "I have never seen anything like it; some of his bones are bent out of shape. I don't understand how a car wreck could cause it. He's going to have to have a lot of operations."

Imagine the look on the good doctor's face when Sherri started laughing. I'll bet he wished he had thrown her out the minute he saw her.

"You do know Bill has Cerebral Palsy?" Sherri tried to explain through her laughter.

"No, no I didn't. But that would make his bent legs make sense," Dr. Rush reasoned.

"That's good, because Bill would really be pissed off if he woke up normal," she told the doctor.

I cannot tell you how hard I laughed when she told me the story. I am glad she waited to tell me until after my ribs healed. She was right about one thing: I would have been pissed if I would have awakened out of a coma and I was normal.

CHAPTER 5

ESCAPE FROM ICU

It was my ninth day in the critical-care unit and it was my last day in the unit. Well almost my last. That's a story I will get into later on. Let me just say, I had a return visit.

Jon and JJ were with me when Dr. Rush made his morning rounds. I always wondered why they called it their "rounds" as he rarely made it to my room before 1 p.m.

"I have a bit of good news for you today, Mr. Chambers," Dr. Rush declared.

"I wish you wouldn't call him Mr. Chambers. All that will do is go to his head," JJ said, cutting in before I could hear what the doctor's good news was. JJ was just kidding of course.

"Alright then Bill, we are going to move you to a floor since you are stable," the doctor continued.

"I don't know about that, Dr. Rush. I don't know if Bill has ever been stable," Jon said getting into the act.

"And these are my good friends," was about all I said looking at the two of them grinning from ear to ear.

Moving to a floor was the best news I had in a while because it meant food and water, no more of those doggone ice chips. I knew it was only hospital food but it sounded pretty good since I hadn't eaten real food in some time. Besides I knew it wouldn't be long before I would talk one of my friends into bringing me a burger. Sure enough, I was chowing down on a Whataburger before the sun went down.

I believe it was Little Jon and his mother who brought it. I call him Little Jon, not because he is the other one's son but because he's about six-five and on the topside of 200 pounds. He was the one standing in line at the chicken cult in my coma.

Little Jon and his mother came to see me four or five times. It is true I do not remember what was talked about but my spirits were always lifted by the time they left.

It was about this time that I finally got in touch with Amanda. I don't remember why it took so long but it was good just to hear her voice. She had hired me one summer to work at a stable complex in Arizona years earlier. She was also the one who talked me into kick starting my writing career.

Amanda was horrified to hear about the accident. It was everything I could do to keep her from jumping on an airplane and coming to see me. I convinced her it would take a while but I would be fine. Amanda called me every night thereafter.

I mention Amanda, Little Jon and his mother here to show how much support and care I received the whole time I was in the hospital. I also know the next time I am doing windshield time, it's going to take a bunch of miles to tell the Lord how grateful I am for all who care for me.

The very first thing they did when I got a real room was to send me for x-rays. This little guy and his helper showed up and moved me to another bed, wheeled me down to x-ray and then put me in a third bed. Now all three of these beds looked just the same and they all had wheels. You see where I am going with this. Why not take me in the bed I was in, in the first place?

I let it slide. You know I figure it was a one-time deal. The very next day the same little guy showed up with his helper for a repeat run down to X-ray. "Hey guys, didn't we just do this yesterday?" I asked. He told me the day before was for my pelvis, now they needed to take pictures of my lungs.

Imagine the look on my face when they showed up the third day. "Now what?" I demanded to know.

This time they wanted an x-ray of my ribs to see how they were healing.

"You just took a picture of my lungs yesterday, aren't my ribs in front of my lungs?" I thought to myself.

Jon came to see me that night. "How are they treating you on this floor?" he wanted to know.

"Alright, I guess. That is when I am actually on this floor. I'll tell you one thing, if I have one more x-ray, I just might glow in the dark. And you don't need to worry about bedsores. I am in and out of more beds than you can shake a stick at. I mean to tell you, I'm in and out of more beds than J. R. Ewing." I let it all go.

I imagine that fell on deaf ears. You see Jon is about 36. I doubt if he knew who J. R. Ewing was. At any rate it was time for my knock-out meds. That is what I called them because I was out like Fraser.

Even though I was out of the ICU unit, the strange, off-the-wall dreams didn't stop. I guess it was all the medication because I never had dreams like that in my life. This is a brief example: One night I played guitar with Stevie Ray Vaughan, and I don't play the guitar

One night I even incorporated two of my favorite people. I, Amanda and Sherri were running a vet clinic. In the dream the clinic had belonged to Sherri's late husband, Gary. Gary had lived in Oklahoma all his life, but for some reason the clinic was in Arizona.

What was really strange was I was doing the doctoring. I know as much about doctoring horses as I do playing guitar. Folks, if you ever drive up to a vet clinic with your horse and you see me coming out with a lab coat on - run. For your horse's sake, run like you hair is on fire.

The best dream I had is a funny story in and of itself. I was in my hospital room entertaining my guests Jeremy and his wife. They are the couple living just down the road from me.

Before I was in the wreck, I let them borrow a book I had written some years back, **The Yellow Outlaw Stud**. It was the first one I did to honor Chris LeDoux's memory.

They were asking about the old horse trainer in the book. I informed them I had named the character after an old college buddy named Bobby Deane. And yes, their names are spelled different for whoever is editing this book. In my book the old horse trainer was Bobby Dean.

About the time I started telling them about my old running buddy, the real Bobby Deane walked through the door.

It felt so good to see my friend that I didn't want to wake up. Bobby and I started telling all the stories from our college years. I mean they were some funny stories. We had Jeremy and his wife laughing at some of the stupid things we did when we were younger men.

Just when I thought my dream couldn't get any better, Susan and Shelly came walking in. For years I've been telling the girls about Bobby Deane, and they read about him in more than one book.

"Susan, Shelly," I said with a toothless smile. Remember my store-bought teeth were lost in the wreck.

"Susan, Shelly this is the famous Bobby Deane. I know he is famous because he has been in a lot books," I said introducing some of my favorite people to one another.

It seems like Bobby and I spent hours telling the girls about our misguided adventures. We would laugh, the girls would laugh and then we would tell them another tale. I don't rightly know if I awoke from my dream after everyone went home or in the middle of the dream. As far as dreams go, it was the best one I had in a while.

I had been home for couple of days when I remembered the dream. I smiled real big, but this time I had teeth. I reached for my phone to call Susan. A dream that good just had to be shared. I started telling her all about this wonderful dream I had and she stops me in the middle, "Bill that wasn't a dream, Bobby did come see you,"

How do you like that? When I was in a coma, I thought being kept in a horse barn was real. When my old friend came to see me, I thought the visit was a dream. No more loopy drugs for me.

Fact or fiction, it can actually be the other way around. Shawn Kelly was a character in two of my murder mysteries. In real life he is a horse farrier and a good friend, despite the fact he went to The Ohio State.

Anyway, just the other day I went by his house to see him. It was the first time I had seen him since I had been home. I remember calling him from the hospital and he and his wife Kris were going to come see me. I thought that he did come see me.

"Shawn, I want thank you and Kris for coming to see me," I said in a grateful tone.

"Bill. I am sorry to say we never made it. There came a big storm that day and we just never made it," my friend informed me.

"Hell Shawn, you could have told me you did and would have never known the difference," I confessed.

I thought I was dreaming when Bobby Deane came to see me, but I wasn't. Then I thought Shawn came to see me and he never did. They must have been some really good drugs. That is all I have to say.

I know for a fact that I was visited by The Wild Man himself. That is what we use to call him when we were growing up. Like I said, everyone had a nickname where I grew up. Mike, in his youth, lived up to ever bit of that name.

Mike was a heartthrob, a fighter and an all-around hell raiser and I was nearly always by his side. I can honestly say every bad habit I had was a direct result of his teachings. It was nearly 40 years ago and I hope we are a little wiser than we were then. As a matter of fact, Mike is now a respected judge in the town where we grew up.

We always said when we were in our eighties we just might revisit our old habits. The plan was to drink, smoke and dip snuff on his front porch. What's it going to do - kill us?

About five months before my wreck, Mike had a massive heart attack. I was seconds away from losing the best friend I ever had. Luckily his wife is an RN and found him just in time. This is one of the reasons I was so surprised to see him during my time of need.

"We need to rethink our plan of falling off the wagon, Chambers." Mike has always called me by my last name. Every now and then he'll call me Billo Crockett, that was my nickname where we grew up.

"I reckon you're right. At this rate neither one of us is going to see 70 let alone 80," I said reading my old friend's mind.

"Well Chambers, are they giving you any good drugs?" my friend asked with a smile.

"Hell yes, it will be just my luck, they'll stick me in rehab after this," I said halfway joking.

"But just think about all the books you'll have to write about this little experience," was his take on the situation.

I guess it was about noon when Mike arrived. By 5 p.m., I was getting a little worried about him. I know Mike. He hates the city, he hates everything about them but nothing more than the traffic.

"Mike, you're lucky it's Saturday. If you leave now, you'll be alright. If you wait too long, the weekend warriors (West Texas speak for drunks) will be out," I warned my friend.

"Do you think I drove all this way to spend a few hours? Hell, I am spending the night," he informed me.

"Where?" I asked because not only does Mike hate the City, he is frugal.

"Right here in this chair," he said in a matter-of-fact way.

"You do remember how mad your wife was that time we went to Arizona?" I tried to remind my friend of his wife's temper.

"Aw, she'll get over it," he assured me. "Besides we are both too beat up to get in much trouble," Mike added with a smile.

Not too long after that Terry, Susan's other brother, and his wife stopped by. I told Mike it would be the perfect time for him to grab a bite to eat and would he grab me a burger while he was out. You figured I would work that in didn't you? I ate so many hamburgers while I was recovering, I will not hardly eat one now.

Terry and his wife Susan agreed to stay with me until Mike came back. My old buddy left me in some pretty good hands. I've always liked spending time with them. Terry always laughs at my stupid jokes and Susan is as sweet as she can be.

It wasn't long before Mike was back, complaining about the traffic. It was Saturday evening. Imagine what he would have been like after spending an hour in rush-hour traffic.

As my memory takes me back some forty years, I stumble on to something I nearly had forgotten. This was not the first time Mike and I had spent the night in a hospital room together. Believe it or not, it was for the very same reason.

It was the winter of 1975 in the small town where we are from. Mike was in the hospital for a heart murmur. You see Mike has always had a bad ticker but it never slowed the Wild Man down.

I braved the cold after school and rode my bicycle to see my best friend. I noticed some more of my other friends were in the small, country-run hospital.

"Damn Mike, it looks like they have everybody up here. The next thing you know I'm going to be in the bed on the other side of you," I should have kept my fool mouth shut, because not twelve hours later there I was, in the bed next to him.

I had gone to a basketball game that night and ran into some older boys. They had been drinking all day and were pretty much drunk.

"Hey Crockett can you drive?" Now what is any 15-year old boy going to say. "Hell yes, I can drive," I boasted.

"Well get your skinny ass in here, and drive us to the beer store," one of the older boys said.

Needless to say, we never made it to the beer store, but true to my word, I woke up right next to Mike. So you see my friends, this was not our first rodeo.

Just the other day I ran into one of those boys who wanted me to drive them to the beer store. Monty is now a grandfather of ten and nearing 60. I don't know how he does it, but he looks like he did thirty years ago.

If you live in West Texas, chances are good you heard the name Monty Jones. While I write about the cowboy life, Monty has lived it for 59 years. This fool even got back in the bucking chute a few years back. I said he was a real cowboy but maybe not a real smart cowboy.

"Hey Crockett, I heard you were in a bad wreck. I hope you're alright now," Monty said in a friendly way.

It dawned on me, this was the first time I had been near death and Monty wasn't involved one way or another.

"At least this time you don't have to hide out from my mother," I joked with my old friend.

Terry and Susan left shortly thereafter. That left Mike and me alone to eat our burgers and talk about days gone by. We use to talk until daylight. That night we were lucky to make it until 10 p.m.

I just thought I was in bad shape. Mike moaned and groaned all night. The next morning, when Dr. Rush was making his rounds, I said he ought to check out my old buddy, "He might be worse off than I am," I kidded.

It was early afternoon when my dear friend left. It touched me knowing he thought of me as I did him. I really don't think one of us could make it without the other. I don't even want to try.

The next day the doctors thought it was time to see if I could put any weight on my legs. I about came unglued with the pain coming from my pelvis. So wouldn't you know it, another round of x-rays were ordered. From there the decision was made to do surgery. The plan was to put three screws in to hold my pelvis together.

The surgery must have worked because from that day to this, I have yet to have any more pain from that region of my body. What they failed to tell me was two of those screws were at least eight inches long.

When they first started talking about putting them in, I thought they were talking about little screws. Just imagine the look on my face when I saw the x-rays and how they baling wired my skinny butt back together.

As is the case with hospitals and me, if something could go wrong, something did go wrong. Everyone, including Susan, Jon, and JJ, told the doctors I was allergic to Hydrocodone. I guess they didn't get the memo.

I have no memory of what happened that night after I was out of recovery. The only accounts I have were relayed to me by my nurse – and they were after the fact.

The story goes I became very agitated and began pulling out all the wires and tubes going in and out of my body. I was demanding my uniform be brought to me. I had to get back to my men on the front. That incident landed my butt back in the ICU unit.

Up until that point, I can halfway explain my off-the-wall dreams, both in out of my coma. But I have no earthly idea where the War II version of General Wild Bill Chambers came from. Maybe too much time watching the History Channel is the best I can figure.

The dream got stranger from there. I was awake that entire night but I was still dreaming. In my mind, I was not in ICU. I was either in hell or the Wizard of Oz.

My male nurse was sitting in front of a control panel with all these knobs and switches. From my vantage point, I couldn't tell if he was the devil or the Wizard himself. I concluded that I was dead and the last two weeks were some kind of tormented dream. I mean I was living on Dean Koontz's plane.

The thought I was dead was shattered by Dr. Rush's face the next day.

"I guess I need to pay a little more mind to what my patients are telling me," he said. But he didn't even know what he said until after he said it. Then he started backtracking after he realized what he had admitted to.

"I mean we tried this new kind of hydrocodone and it seems you are allergic to that as well," the good doctor said after he had collected his thoughts.

Before long they returned me to the floor I was on. I began my apology tour after I heard what I had done the night before. I started with the nurse who informed me of my actions. To their credit, everyone told me they knew the guy they saw the night before wasn't the real me. Yes I was a pain-in-the-ass patient, but I was no head case.

Before I end this chapter, I would like to note, I received the best of care from Harris Methodist Hospital. Their medical staff was second to none. I don't know if I would be here today if not for the hard-working people who make up the staff at this fine hospital. I thank them for their patience and all those who came to see me. More to the point, I thank them for my care.

CHAPTER 6

I WANT TO GO BACK TO MY HORSE STALL

I don't remember when I first heard them talking about discharging me. Me and my drug-induced self was more than likely dancing a jig; maybe not on a dance floor, but in my head. I confused discharge with going home.

I live alone with my critters, not to mention out in the middle of nowhere. I mean my town is so small, if you could call it a town. It doesn't even have a zip code. There I was, not two days out of getting my body screwed back together, and I think I am going home. What planet was I living on? I could barely hold my head up.

It was about that time I heard the word, "rehab" floated about.

"You see Jon, I told you they were giving me too many drugs; now I have go dry out," I said jokingly.

"They are not talking that kind of rehab. They're talking more about a place where you can get therapy so you can go home," he said to me.

What Jon and some folks didn't know was I spent many years in therapy for my Cerebral Palsy. I have been stretched more times than Stretch Armstrong. I think I was the prototype for that popular toy.

Sometimes knowledge is a dangerous thing. I was thinking I could go home and do therapy on myself and why wouldn't I? Hell, I was "three sheets to the wind" anyway. Drugs have a way of convincing a person they can do anything. Thank the Good Lord, there were other people there doing the thinking for me.

Not everyone was completely sold on the therapy deal right off. Sherri wanted to take me home with her and take care of me. On the face of it, it sounded pretty good to me, but Sherri had a job. She couldn't take care of me any more than I could but I love her for the thought.

The decision was made I would go to rehab. Then the question became where? There wasn't just a whole lot of time to figure it out as the hospital was discharging me. Neither me nor any of my friends had a lot of experience in such matters. I don't even know why I put myself in the mix. I was so full of pain meds, I didn't know which way was up.

Jon and JJ found a place where they live, in Whitesboro. Jon had received a good sales pitch. He then came to the hospital to sell me on the idea. We both bought into it - hook, line and sinker.

The selling point for me, as well as Jon, was that it was a top-notch center. That was the first lie they sold us on. They said I would have a private room. That was not a lie, although my closet back home was bigger than the room.

The good points that Jon sold me on were true. If I were to go there, I would be within ten miles of the Double J Ranch and they were only a phone call away. JJ's dad, her stepmom, and her mother were also close by for added support. And the cherry on top was my college pal, Zach, was close as well. So I bought in - sight unseen.

The night before I left to go to this rehab center, I had another one of my crazy dreams. In my dream I saw this nice home with trees all around it. When I went inside, I saw a number of others folks either on crutches or in wheelchairs. The home had a warm feeling about it.

"I can do this, it will not be that bad," I said to myself in the dream.

The next day was my discharge. I figured Jon would pick me up and we would drive out to this rehab center. While I waited, I tried to picture just where this place was.

I was no stranger to the city of Whitesboro. I had even written a book with the setting being in that town. I kept racking my brain but I still couldn't remember seeing a rehab center.

I was starting to get worried when Jon wasn't there to pick me up by 4 p.m. The nurse came in a little after 4 p.m. and said my ride was there.

"Well tell Jon to come get me, I can't walk down there," I said to the nurse.

"It is not your friend Mr. Chambers, it's an ambulance," the nurse informed me.

"What's up with that, he didn't think I could ride an hour in the pickup," I asked.

"It is policy for most of these centers that the patient arrive by ambulance," the nurse informed me once again.

I should have known something was up after hearing the nurse's answer. Perhaps I would have if not for all the medication I was on.

"Alright, let's get this show on the road," was my only response.

These two guys, straight out of the Gum Ball Rally, show up with a gurney to load me. This is no lie. They take me to a 1990-something conversion van that has been converted one last time to an ambulance. I know this because it still had the shag carpet everywhere.

But that wasn't the weird part at all. They get me loaded up and we get on the road before these two guys realize they have no clue where Whitesboro is. So from back on the gurney, I'm giving these guys directions. I often ask myself, would they have listened to me if they knew how much pain meds I was on. Regardless, I managed to get the three of us there in one piece.

They drove up to this so-called rehab center and pulled me out of the back. In an instant, I know where I am at and it's no rehab center.

"Hey boys, we got the wrong place, this is an old-folk's home," I alerted the surfer dudes.

"No Mr. Chambers, this is the address we were given," Shaggy said.

"If this is the right address, then you can take me back to where you found me," I told them.

"We cannot do that, Mr. Chambers," Scooby chimed in.

By then the people from the old-folk's home were out to receive their youngest, most irate patient. From the get-go, they tried to go back on their word when they put me in a room with someone else. I put my foot down, I was promised a private room and I was damn sure going to get one. I put in a call to Jon faster than you can say, "pissed off."

I guess Jon knew I was fit to be tied because it didn't him hardly any time to get down there. I explained myself as plainly as I could to my friend and he left to talk to whoever was in charge. Meanwhile I watched my new roommate talk to those no longer among us, or were never with us.

Jon came back in a half hour and began to explain to me that it was a retirement home as well as a rehab. He also said I would get a private room the next day. By then my meds were working their way out of my system, I was in a lot of pain.

"You need to give Bill his medication and let him sleep, he'll be more agreeable in the morning" I overheard him tell the charge nurse.

"We do not have his medication as of yet," she told Jon.

"What do mean you don't have his medication, the doctor sent the order to the drug store yesterday and the drug store is right across the street. How can you not have his meds?" said Jon who by then was getting a little hot.

"We are not allowed to use any pharmacy but our own and Mr. Chambers' medication is not here yet," she informed him.

"I don't care where you get his medication but you better get him some quick. I'll yank him out of here and have a team of lawyers down here by sun up," he said. It doesn't pay to piss an Arkansas hillbilly off, especially if he is married to Arkansas royalty.

It didn't take the charge nurse any time at all to round me up a pain pill as well as a sleeping pill. That was the beginning of my sixteen days in hell. By the time my stay was half over, I was missing my horse stall in a barn that was in my coma.

The 6 a.m. the next morning, I was getting ready to take the first shower I had since May 3. Up until that morning it had all been spit bathes given to me by aids at the hospital. I had been medicated out the ying yang and flat on my back for weeks so I had no idea what shape my body was in.

They put me in a wheelchair made from PVC pipe then they pushed me into this huge shower stall. It looked like a carwash for old people to me. Then this aid tried to scrub me down like a show calf. I thought I had never been humiliated in my life but the best was yet to come.

I looked down at my naked body and I was horrified. I was emaciated from the top down. I was never overweight. I was always a little skinny but this had passed skinny some time ago. My legs and arms had no muscle tone at all. I didn't know whose list I was on but I looked like I had just walked out of a concentration camp. Right then was a do-or-die time for me.

I could cry about it or I could do something about it. Momma raised me to not be a crybaby. Even if I wanted to give up, she would have reached out from the grave and kicked my behind.

Somehow I came up with a set of dumb bells and my recovery began that day. Anyone who might have thought I was down for the count really didn't know me at all.

Believe me when I say I heard, "You'll never be what you were before the wreck," more than once. All that did was piss me off. In a strange way, I set out to prove them right. I was determined I would not be like I was before my accident - I would be better. What they didn't know was that I had been fighting the same fight all my life. I was a little rusty but the Lord had put the grit in me at birth and I would finish the race better than I had started it.

The first day I was there, I met my therapist. She had a PhD and I really liked her. In another setting we could have set the world on its ear. But she was confined by the system she found herself in. You see rehab in there wasn't the rehab I had grown up with. It was more or less set up on the quota system.

By all rights I should have not done any therapy until my bones had healed and what therapy I had was either tapping my toes or working my upper body, neither of which was the problem. I couldn't walk was the problem that needed to be fixed.

I say quota system because rain or shine, whether or not I was toilet-hugging sick, she came and got me every day so they could charge the insurance for a day's worth of therapy. She admitted as much to me on one of my last days there. I think in a different place she would have been one hell of a therapist. I hope someday she can find the right setting to prove me right. You see she was like me - trapped by the system.

I had a second visitor that first day, by a speech therapist. This young girl and I clashed from the get go. My accident had broken my bones and had crushed my chest. It had caused a lot of damage, but it had nothing to do with my speech. The whole concept of sending me to a speech therapist because I could not walk was stupid.

This girl must have been fresh out of college with her head full of theory. From jump street, she took it on herself to correct the one thing that I felt wasn't broken. It is true that I talk with a bit of a slur and at times I know I am hard to understand. I feel like I have perfected my slur and was quite happy with my speech. I told her as much that first encounter.

What did she do? She pulled rank on me. Jon had power of attorney over me so she called him and JJ in for a sit down meeting with me. That is what really pissed me off. I was over 50 years of age and this young girl is going to treat me like a 10-year-old and call momma and daddy. I don't think so.

I can honestly say this was the only time I defied Jon outright. I had a 20 some-odd years of speech therapy to get to the point I am happy with. If I thought she could have made me better I would have bought into it. But her new-fangled tricks were not so new to me. They were the same rehashed therapies that I had tried decades earlier.

What it came down to was the quota system again. This time I wasn't playing. The powers that be were not going to lock me into a useless therapy so they could add that to my bill. Finally they got the hint and stopped coming for me for speech therapy.

Being inside an old folks' home really opened my eyes to its dishonest nature. Now to be fair, I am not painting the entire industry with the same brush. But this home for the elderly was nothing short of a scam.

The longer I was a resident, the more things I saw things that were just wrong. I wasn't their normal patient. I wasn't talking to people who weren't there. My body had gone to hell in a hand basket but my mind was still intact. I saw things that would make your toes curl.

There were also things I didn't see - like a doctor. Two thirds of the time that I was there, I was sick, and I am not a sickly person. One night I was having chest pains. Did they call a doctor? Hell no. They sent me by ambulance to Sherman. Some more wasted health-care dollars.

I never had a doctor there see me or anyone else for that matter. It begs the question, "Just who was writing all the prescriptions or the doctor's orders?" Can you do that without ever seeing the person? It all seems a bit shady to me.

The food they feed these poor people wouldn't pass as slop. I spent two years eating what they called food in college and this stuff was worse times ten. They were more than likely billing four-star prices for food a hog wouldn't eat.

I was lucky I had a cell phone and the ranch on speed dial. I ate very little from their kitchen since the boys would bring me anything Whitesboro had to offer in the way of fast food. Two or three times a week, Jean, JJ's stepmom, would bring a home-cooked meal. JJ's dad would come by every day with a milk shake.

I have to give credit where credit is due. If it wasn't for Garrett and the boys at the Double J Ranch, Rick and Jean, Jon and JJ footing my fast-food bills, I might have starved. It is said that it takes a village to raise a child. I'm here to say it takes a ranch to feed one skin-and-bones writer.

The people who made up the staff at the rest home were a mixed bag. Some looked like the dregs off the streets of Whitesboro. You could tell this was the only game in town for them. It seemed like once a week one would get fired for coming to work high or drunk.

On the other end of the spectrum, there were those who had real compassion. It was a calling more than a job for these few. One comes to mind. He was a Mexican boy about 21 years of age. Louis wiped my butt when I was too sick to. He fed me when my hands couldn't hold a fork. He never bitched about a task. The boy just loved his job and I loved him for it.

But my favorite was a lady named Brenda. She was from the horse world just as I was. She knew from the moment Shaggy and Scooby dumped me at the door, just who I was. She had seen me at horse shows clowning around with her boss, old Jack. He was just like my beloved Bob Kurtz, the last of the breed.

Brenda was working two jobs: the morning shift at the so-called retirement home, and in the evenings she still worked for Jack. I cannot tell you what it meant to me having her there. We would talk about the old days, horses or anything to keep my mind off the fix I was in. I don't know if I would have made it through it without Brenda

The first thing I did when I could drive and had a new car was to go see her. I wanted to thank her for helping me through the darkest part of my recovery.

I guess by now you know why I named this chapter as I did. By the end of the first day, I was ready to be put back in my horse stall.

CHAPTER 7

WILD BILL'S FORGETTABLE ADVENTURE

I guess I got on my soap box a bit in the last chapter. I described the place I was sent to in a not-too-flattering way. In this chapter I will tell what the place was like after my first day and let me tell you, it was some rollercoaster ride.

I stayed in my room at the rest home most of the time except when they would wheel me out to do some useless therapy. If I was awake, I was working out with my dumb bells or exercising my legs. I used what I had learned growing up at the West Texas Rehab Center. This was and is one of the finest rehab centers in the world, started back in the '50s by some rich cattle ranchers. This top-notch center doesn't charge a dime either. Most of what I am today, I owe to them.

Bill Snow was the man in charge of the therapy department back in the '70s and '80s, the man who saw to it that everyone received the best treatment possible. Bill took an interest in a 10-year-old boy with braces on his legs.

"If you could do anything little man, what would it be?" was the first question he asked me.

"That's easy. Get shed of these braces, and wear some cowboy boots," was the answer from 10-year-old me.

Do you want to know something? Within six months, the braces were gone and a new pair of cowboy boots had taken their place. Except for a few years in the late '70s, I have been wearing them ever since. If you are wondering - yes I had a pair of platform shoes in the late '70s. You just think I walk funny now.

With Bill Snow in my ear, I set upon the task of making myself whole again. His spirit and my will pushed me on there in my little room in the old folk's home. It didn't matter what was going on in the outside world, the ten-by-ten room became my world.

I really don't know how long I had been there when my Sherri came to see me. It must have been in those first few days because I was still heavily medicated. I didn't even remember the visit until she reminded me about the tornado, then it all came back to me.

"How do you forget about a tornado?" you might ask. The answer, "They were some mighty powerful drugs."

She said we were talking one minute and in the hall the next minute. I must have been a really lucky man. First, I survive the mother of all car wrecks. I then survive a tornado with a beautiful blonde and a hall full of the elderly. What can I say? It has been a strange year.

Sherri was like I was. She wasn't real happy about the place. It wasn't what she was told. If you remember a few chapters ago, she wanted me to go home with her. I can see now that wouldn't have worked much better. Sherri's love for me is so deep that she would have spoiled me.

I know me. I love female attention. I would still be there lapping it up like gravy. One thing, I wasn't going to get where I was by being spoiled. I had to get pissed off so I could get better. Believe me, I was pissed off the whole time I was there but if that is what it took, that's okay.

Do you remember my shower scene from the last chapter? I was humiliated but I was also mad. Within a few days, I was giving myself a shower without any help. When I get angry I get motivated. It is just the way I was built.

Sherri didn't come see me anymore after that. I know it hurt her to see me in a place like that. I could hear it in her voice each night when she would call. I will say there were a few times when she offered to come get me when I thought I was at the end my rope. As a friend, or even a sister, it doesn't get any better than that.

Shortly after Sherri's visit, I took myself off of the heavy drugs. I knew if I waited on the rest home, they would take their sweet time about it - especially when they were charging $10 a pop. Drugs are more than likely cheaper on the street. From then on, it was non-narcotic pain relievers and a sleeping pill at night.

There were some withdrawals after weeks of sedation but I had expected as much. I guess that was the first time I really got sick. It didn't matter how bad I felt, I was still in my cubbyhole pumping iron. In my condition, pumping iron was three pounds at a time. But it was all day, every day.

Jon waited until the drugs were out of my system before he brought my newly acquired lawyer to see me. In the beginning we thought the people who hit me had insurance and I had lawyers coming out of the woodwork. I was getting calls from law offices every day.

I was in no shape to pick one so I let Jon do the picking. He conferred with the legal minds representing Tyson Chicken and came up with Mr. Ed Wright. To hear him tell it, he was one of the best when it came to tort. That was after he told us his life's story. I kind of felt sorry for Jon because I knew it was the second time he had heard it.

The man's story went on and on, from his high-school days of being a track star to the overweight, middle-aged man I saw before me. Being the smart ass I am, I figured I would cut the ice with a lawyer joke. That is when I got the chance to speak. To his credit, he let out a loud belly laugh. Now I don't know if it was a fake laugh or not. With lawyers, there is no way to be sure.

He came to see me two more times at the so-called rehab center. Each time telling me how hard he was going to fight for me and with my case he couldn't lose. Well granddaddy always said a lawyer was a lot like certain women.

"They'll whisper anything you want to hear, as long as they think a payday is coming," he would say.

Anyway while he was doing whatever he was doing, I was researching the Texas tort laws. Most folks don't know them boys in Austin gave the insurance companies one hell of a sweetheart deal. If a person buys the minimum policy, the insurance is only required to pay out $30,000 for bodily harm and $25,000 for property damage. Like I said earlier, my little ride in the helicopter was $32,000 by itself. Things were not adding up in my favor and each time the lawyer would come see me, I would quiz him on such matters.

"Are you sure you're not a lawyer," he would ask me after one of our sessions. I felt like telling him, "No, because I have a conscious," but I didn't. It always pays to know what the lawyer knows.

Granddaddy was right. That lawyer dropped me like a hot potato when he found out the person who hit me gave the officer a bogus insurance card. I mean the man wouldn't even entertain other ideas. Now I don't feel so bad about telling my lawyer joke. In fact, I wish I would have told more of them.

If my lawyer was the greatest lawyer in the world, I still would doubt if such a thing exists. I did however have one of the finest dentists I have ever seen.

About six weeks before the accident, I had what was left of my upper teeth pulled and got some dentures put in. I was tired of looking like some toothless hick from the hills after my fall in the winter. I was just getting used to them when the wreck occurred.

My dentist heard I had lost them in the accident. He came every week on his own time and took molds of my mouth, right there in my little room. By the time I was released, he had a new set ready. The man never charged me a dime for any of it. I can't thank him enough for going beyond the call of duty.

Even though it rained nearly every day I was in my tiny room, there were some rays of light. It was a strange spring. We had our annual rainfall by June. It rained over twenty inches in May alone. It was like the floodgates just opened up after being welded shut for so long.

My first ray of sunshine came from a lifelong friend. Kevin and his wife Tammye came to see me one weekend. Kevin and I live about ten miles from each other, just like when we were kids. As a matter of fact, he was one of the first to see me when I wrecked some forty years earlier.

"Where is my roll of snuff and typewriter?" I felt like saying. You see that is what he brought me all those years ago. But I no longer dip snuff and they haven't made a typewriter in at least twenty years. So what would be the point other than it being funny as all get out.

Susan told me Kevin was one of the first persons she called. That seems fitting since he had known me the longest. I don't know how many visits he made to the hospital. I can't say I remember one. But that's on me, because I was heavily medicated.

We've talked several times since I've been home. From what I can gather, he was one of the first ones there. He said it was touch-and-go for a few days, meaning I was on death's doorstep.

It was good to see him and his wife at my new digs. Mainly because I knew I would remember the visit. I don't know what we talked about or how long they stayed, the fact that they came is really all that matters.

My birthday fell on a Saturday this year and I really wasn't looking forward to it. There's something about having a birthday at an old folks' home just sounds depressing. Maybe it wouldn't sound that bad if I was turning 85, but I was turning 55 – totally a horse of a different color.

To be real honest, I was hoping I would sleep through the day completely. But that is not the way the cards fell. First Jon and JJ showed up with flowers, then here come Rick and Jean with a sketchpad and color pencils. It was something I had been wanted to help pass the time.

They had no sooner left the room when Brandon walked through the door. It was one thing for him to come to see me at the hospital, because the hospital wasn't that far. It had to take him at least a couple hours to make the drive to Whitesboro. That is after he drove the three hours from Abilene the day before. For him to do all of that to come see me - well it really touched me.

I would say Brandon was a good kid but he hadn't been a kid for some time. Brandon is a grown man with a hell of a future ahead of him. He is an engineer and runs his own division at the firm. Last year he bought a new house in Buffalo Gap. I couldn't be more proud of him if he was my own son.

Brandon had a bit of good news to deliver. His mother, grandmother and Shelly were also coming later on that day.

"Maybe it was going to be a good birthday after all," I remember thinking to myself. It had sure started out that way.

Brandon and I spoke for the better part of an hour. Back then I was thinking that I was getting a settlement, so we talked about the new Ford F-150s. He had just bought one completely dressed out. I knew back then that it was pie in the sky, but it never hurts to dream a little.

I told Brandon it was time for him to go enjoy the rest of the weekend instead of hanging out with this old man in a rest home. I know because I was 30 once upon a time. He had made my day; it was time to make his.

Brandon was no sooner out the door when my cell phone rang. It was his mother, Susan.

"Bill, Shelly's truck will not start," was what she told me. My heart sunk like a stone after hearing those few words. I thought about asking for my sleeping pill a little early. It seemed as though my birthday had come to an end.

An hour passed like a day as my spirits sank. I was fixing to pull the plug on my 55th birthday when a knock came at the door. I figured it was one of the staff members wanting something. Imagine my surprise to find Susan, her mom and Shelly on the other side of the door.

"I thought you said you were not coming," I said, as was surprised.

"No, all I said was Shelly's truck wouldn't start. You see you never listen to me," Susan said with Chester-cat grin.

All in all it wasn't a bad birthday. If it wasn't for the place I was in, it might have been one of the best. I slept good that night, knowing I was loved.

My birthday was the best day I had while I was at the old folks' home. A few weeks later, my worst day would arrive. I really can't say what started my downhill slide into a deep depression. I think it was a combination of certain factors that broke the camel's back.

Jon and JJ had been out of town for a week. Zach had gone to work baling hay. Garrett was spending more and more time with his girlfriend. The only one I really saw much of was Rick, JJ's daddy. It was hard for anyone to come up from home during the week. I guess I was getting lonely; that had to be part of it.

I had been sick for over a week. It seemed like everything I ate came right back up. It got to the point where I was barely eating anything at all. In fact, just the mere thought of food gagged me. It was something that just drug on for what seemed forever. I was already under weight. It wasn't good for me to stop eating.

The third thing was I was homesick really bad. I had been gone for nearly two months. I was missing my dogs and other critters. All I wanted to do was go home.

Add all these things together and my world grew to be a very dark place. I knew I had to find my way out of the depression. One night I hatched a grand scheme - or it sounded good at the time. You see, even though I was off the pain medication, I still wasn't thinking clearly. The next morning I was going to make my move.

I put in a call to the before-mentioned West Texas Rehab Center. They remembered me after all the years that had passedt. I told them what had happened and they agreed to see me. I knew they didn't have in-patient care but I didn't see where I needed it.

Then I put in a call to Nancy because I knew I needed a place to stay while I was going to the center for therapy. I told her I would only be there three days a week. The rest of my week would be spent at my place.

"Can you drive, Bill?" was the first question she asked.

"Sure I can drive, and I still have the Town Car," I informed her. It sounded good and I actually thought I could drive, even though I couldn't put two steps together.

The third call I made was to my neighbor. I told Emily my great escape plan and asked her if she would mind stocking the fridge for me. I didn't think I could get around the store on my own. You See, I did know a few of my limitations.

What I didn't know was as soon as I hung up both of these ladies were calling Jon to see what in the world was going on. He had no idea what I was up to but he was bound to find out.

There were just a few things I hadn't figured on. First, I had no idea that either one of these ladies knew Jon, let alone had his cell number. The second was I didn't even know Jon was back in town. Wild Bill's great escape was headed for a snag.

By midday my little hair-brained idea was coming together - or so I thought. Then all of a sudden the door flew open and there stood Jon. The man is hard core and old school, just as I am. The only difference is I had twenty more years to knock the rough edges off. Everyone calls it wisdom; I just think life sands the rough places down.

"Where in the hell do you think you are going? I got half of Texas calling me, wondering if you are able to care of yourself," he said in angry voice.

"Damn it Jon, this place is killing me. This is not a rehab; this is where people go to die. Did you smell that odor coming down the hall? That is the smell of death. If am going to die, I am going to do it at my house, on my terms," I said as I got my back hairs up.

"Don't give me that shit, you are not dying," he fired back.

"What do you know? Every day I am here, I die a little more. Or worse, I have become something I am not. Yes I am crippled but I am not a cripple. Every day I am here, I become something I fought all my life not to become.

"So today I took matters into my own hands, I called the only place I know that works," I said busting out in tears. I am not a person who cries, that is not my shtick.

"But why do you have to call everybody you know?" my friend blurted out. "Why can't you call and tell me? You don't think I know this is a dive, I am not stupid."

I was such an emotional wreck that it was hard to comprehend what he was trying to say. All I knew was I wanted out. I damn near curled up and disappeared. At that point I wanted to.

I think he knew that and began to tell me about a place he had found.

"Bill it's a real rehab, I swear. It is in Sherman. I drove past it last night. I'll go look at it today and talk to them," he said as he tried to console me.

"And if that doesn't work?" I said through my tears.

"If that doesn't work, I'll get you a nurse and move you to the ranch," he offered.

He talked to the people and the next day he took me and I talked to them. But they wouldn't take me until the doctor said I could put weight on my legs without injuring my pelvis again.

No one knew how long that would be - maybe three months. I just knew I was going back to the rehab place and I did - for one more weekend. Jon assured me he just needed a few days to get things in order. As long as there was light at the end of the tunnel, I could do three more days.

Jon was true to his word and three days later, he and my lawyer came and picked me up. I would say the happiest day of my life was when they wheeled me out of that "hell on earth," but that day was yet to come.

CHAPTER 8

AT THE DOUBLE J RANCH

I knew that the worst of my recovery was in the rear-view mirror when I entered the main gate of the Double J Ranch. I realized my work had just begun but the mental and the depressing part was over. The darkness had lifted and the future lay in front of me.

I was still underweight, still in a wheel chair and pretty much the same as I was the day before but I had hope. I always had hope but the longer I was in the home, the more my hope began to dim. It is true what they say about your surroundings. They sure can affect your mindset. Like Jimmy Buffett said, "Changes in latitudes, changes in attitudes,"

Yes, I waited until halfway through the book until I quoted Jimmy. It surprises even me.

The first thing I did after arriving on the ranch was to go see everyone down at the barn. Terry and his wife were the only ones I hadn't seen since the wreck. Terry has a thing about hospitals and nursing homes. I can't say I blame him. I wouldn't be there unless I had no choice - and I had none.

I have known Terry since my early days on the horse show circuit. We made it an art by jacking with each other.

"Hey you grumpy old man, you still alive Sartan?" was how I greeted my dear friend.

"What the hell are you doing out, you crazy-ass cripple?" Terry fired back.

I knew after hearing his words that the world was right. I also knew by the look in his eyes, he had been concerned about me.

The next person was the newcomer to the ranch. Brian had been laid off at the paper mill in Arkansas. He had moved to Texas to try his hand with horses. I knew after watching him in the arena that he was a born horseman.

I had met him and his family years earlier at a roping. He and Jon had nearly walked away with the whole shooting match that night. I would run into Brian at least once a year since we first met.

Even though I had seen him here and there, I really didn't know him very well. I got to know him in the weeks that followed and I am so glad I did. Brian is a man of few words but his actions speak volumes. In short, I do not know if I have ever met I finer human being. And I have never met I single person who loved Whataburger more. Yes Brian, I am telling on you.

I had to look real hard to find Garrett but there at the back of the barn, I saw him and Jose mucking out stalls.

"I hope they're not cleaning one out for me," I joked to myself.

"Hey boys, I'd come give you a hand, but my chair hasn't arrived yet," I said, joking with them.

"We will wait on the chair," Garrett fired back as he laid his stall fork down and walked toward me.

Jose didn't say anything. He doesn't understand my English and that has nothing to do with his nationality. He always just smiles real big like he knows what I am saying but I know he doesn't have a clue. I asked Jon about it once.

"Jose's English isn't too good," he said trying to explain.

"If that was the case, he ought to know every word I am saying," I replied.

"How do you figure?" Jon wanted to know.

"Hell, my English isn't that good either," was my punch line. Jon laughed a long time after that gag.

He still tells the story from time to time. Jon took me up to the main house after I said hello to everyone and "pulled their chains" a little. By then lunch had arrived and I was hungry. It wasn't my first time at the ranch. I knew if I wanted something to eat, I better get it before the boys came up from the barn.

It had been an eventful morning, a little more action than I was used to at the home. I never thought I'd be using the term, "at the home." I guess you never know. Like I was say, my morning had been full so it was time for a nap.

This was the first time I had recovered from something at the Double J Ranch, not even the first time that year. I had been there a week at the beginning of spring when they pulled the rest of my upper teeth. Like an old man, I made tracks to my room.

Later on that evening, I wheeled myself down to the barn. I knew Jon and JJ kept all their exercise equipment in the barn's office. I wanted to see if they had anything I could use.

"Stationary bike - nope not ready for that yet. Stair climber - damn sure not there either," I said to myself as I looked for anything I could use.

I suddenly saw just what I was looking for in the furthest reaches of the room. It was a set of dumb bells, a little bigger than what I had been using at the home, but I had outgrown the old ones anyway.

The barn's office was hot so I retrieved the weights and went back into the part of the barn where there was a breeze. Garrett and Allen, the farrier, were shoeing a horse in the alleyway. I talked to them while I was pumping the iron I had found.

It was the first thing I found to be different. I could actually have a conversation with people whenever I wanted. I didn't have to wait for someone to come see me. It wasn't like I could roll down the hall and talk to another patient.

I went to bed that night with a good feeling. I wasn't home yet, but I was one step closer. The road isn't so long if you can see the end of it and believe me, I had the end in my sights.

The next day was filled with interviews and I was the one being interviewed. Jon had lined out all kinds of people in the medical field to come see what my needs were. At the end of the day, I had a home nurse, an aid and two therapists.

The ball was starting to bounce my way and just in time. The start of horse-show season was kicking in, just like it does every year. In my condition, it didn't mean a lot. I was out for the season but Jon and JJ were not. They were fixing to get on the road but they made sure I was in good hands before they did. I would have Garrett and Brian around at night and my new medical team during the day.

I also had Jean cooking for me and Rick chasing down milkshakes, I might have gotten sick of hamburgers but never anything to do with ice cream. If I had a beach, life would have been perfect.

You know how they say, "When it rains it pours?" I found out it can be true about anything. It all happened before Jon and JJ left for a show.

Zach, my old college buddy called me one night and said he had a Hoveround I could use. Not too long before that, my neighbor, Mike Kaz, who you will meet later, said they had one I could use.

The next morning, Sherri called and said she was fixing her late sister's Hoveround for me. If that was not enough, Ramona, who is JJ's mom, called and said she had bought not one, but two, at Goodwill for me. They needed batteries but that was nothing.

Two questions came to mind. The first was when was it going to stop raining Hoverounds? The second was what was the richest woman in North Texas doing in Goodwill? At any rate, I had enough Hoverounds to start a dealership.

Shortly after the Hoveround flood, Jon and JJ left for Mexico. So that left the boys and me holding down the ranch. Garrett was assigned to help me around the house plus he had to take me to Fort Worth for a doctor's appointments. That is where I saw my opening.

At that point, it had been several weeks since I had been home. I was homesick in the worst way. You never think a piece of dirt can mean that much unless it's your piece of dirt and you've been gone awhile. It wasn't only my little ranch. It was all the critters that called it home. I was missing them more than the place.

My doctor's appointment was after lunch so I talked Garrett into stopping by my place for some clothes. I knew I didn't need the clothes, I doubted if they would fit anyway. I did however need to see my place and my critters. I had to see what I was working for - the light at the end of the tunnel, if you will. Garrett agreed to stop by the ranch without much pleading on my part.

It was nearing mid-summer and it was hot. All the rain we had that year made you feel like you were on the coast. You could cut the humidity with a butter knife. I had given Garrett a way out of a hot barn and he was all over it like sand on the beach.

I awoke about 4 a.m. My body was electrified with the prospect of going home, even if it was only for a visit. I tried my best not to wake anyone while I got ready. There was a fat chance of that happening, the boys of the Double J sleep like the dead.

By 6 a.m., I was ready to roll but I was the only one. Garrett Mise is by far the hardest person in the world I have ever tried to wake up. He is even harder to get moving once he's awake. It took a good two hours to get the lad in the car. He just didn't seem to understand that he was cutting into my home time. I knew I couldn't stay but I wanted every last minute I could get on my own piece of dirt.

An hour later we were driving through my front gate. Tears filled my eyes just knowing I was home. My yard dog Z ran up the drive to greet us. She was a sight for sore eyes. In the background I could hear the rest of the herd barking. Even the donkeys seemed to be singing a welcome song.

My yard and pastures were freshly mowed. I just knew Mike Kaz had a hand in it. Then when the front porch came into view, my suspicions were confirmed. The front of my house looked like a construction project that only Mike could pull off.

Two-inch drill pipe, tools and a cement mixer blocked the front door. You see it wasn't real clear to anyone but me if I'd ever walk again. Mike, being the Saint he is, was going to make sure I could get into my own house - just not that day.

Mike was building a ramp on to my porch, and not just any ramp. It was one like you might find at a federal building or a loading dock.

Mike Kaz has never done anything half-assed in his life. Furthermore, I believe he has a place in heaven waiting on him even if he doesn't spend another minute in church. That is just what kind of a person he is. I lucked out when I moved in next to him and his wife.

I jumped, or the best I could jump, into my old golf cart. Z, my trusty mutt, was there in a blink of an eye. She was just as happy to see me as I was to see her. I had to send Garrett inside the house just so he wouldn't see me cry.

"I couldn't get up the back steps and Kaz has fixed it so I cannot get in the front," I told Garrett. "I need you to get me a pair of boots, some shirts, and for heaven's sake grab me a cowboy hat. I have been too long without one. I'm going down to the kennels to see Tater and the rest of the pack. If you don't mind, give me a minute with my dogs - it's been a spell."

Down at the kennels the tears began to flow as each dog ran to me. But they were tears of joy not of sadness. I was beginning to wonder if I would ever see my dogs again, but see them I did. They were all fat and sassy and happy to see the old man. Mike had been feeding them well and I was, and will always be, grateful to Kaz for that.

I don't really know how long I was at the kennels but it didn't seem near long enough. Soon I saw Garrett coming out the back door with what I had sent him for. I petted each dog once more before turning the golf cart around and heading back to the car. By then the tears had all dried up and I was smiling ear to ear.

Garrett was about to load my things in the back seat when I grabbed my hat away from him.

"Now I am fully dressed," I said as I mashed it down on my head.

I left the home place as happy as a lark. The young lad from Arkansas had made my day and I sure did thank him for it. What he didn't know and I forgot to tell him was my place was just the start. Old men are crafty that way.

"I need to stop at the bank when we go through town," I informed the boy.

"The bank," he fired back at me.

"Yes the bank and a few other places. Don't sweat it, we have plenty of time," I pointed out.

There is nothing in the world like a small-town bank. Jennifer, the bank manager, had spent about an hour reading my mail to me over the phone just a few days earlier. The cards and get-well wishes really touched my heart. Not to mention the fact she had taken time out of her day to read them to me. Try finding that at a big-city bank.

Everyone stopped what they were doing when Garrett wheeled me into the bank. You would think we were there to rob the joint if you didn't know any better.

Each person came from out behind their desk to welcome me home. At the end of the line was Jennifer with the biggest hug I had received in some time. I would be lying if I said it didn't feel good to be home again. Garrett didn't know what to think. I guess he had never seen people at a bank act like that. Like I said, there is nothing like a small-town bank

On the way to the car, I told him I had one last stop to make. "All right, where?" the young man asked.

"Down the road there is a hamburger place. I need to run by there for just a second," I tried to explain.

"We just ate before we left town, what is it with you and hamburgers? I swear sometimes I think you and Brian are brothers," Garrett told me.

"I know we just ate. I am not going there to eat. I have to pick up some footballs. And no, I am not related to the Whataburger Kid," I informed the boy.

I had Wade send the Tony Romo autographed footballs to another college buddy who lived close to me. Earlier that morning, while I was waiting on Garrett, I had put in a call to Dr. David Lowe. David is another character from a couple of my murder mysteries. I guess by now you see a pattern, and if I know you, chances are you will find yourself in one of my books.

I asked David if he would run the footballs by Giant Burger on his way to the office. I knew chances were good that he was going to have breakfast there anyway. Mason, the man who owned the burger joint, had been a trusted friend to both David and me. In fact, most of the time that is how we passed messages to each other.

"Let me get this straight. You want to go to a hamburger stand to pick up two Tony Romo autographed footballs and not for a burger. You are one of a kind Wild Bill Chambers," Garrett said, sounding almost amused.

"Exactly," was all I had to say.

I knew Garrett really didn't want to pull the wheelchair out of the trunk again, so I sent him in to retrieve my Dallas Cowboy stash. The very next thing I knew, Mason and most of his workers were surrounding the car. They all wanted to come see how I was getting along.

"Don't go anywhere, I have the cook making you a few burgers for the road," Mason informed me.

It wasn't long before we were headed toward Fort Worth's Cow Town with the burger and football. I could tell Garrett was somewhat amazed by the welcome we received at every stop on our journey. The one thing the lad didn't know - so was I.

We got ourselves lost a few times before finding the doctor's office. I swear that boy cannot follow directions, but with five minute to spare, we were sitting in the office filling out paper work. It wasn't long before my name was called and we left the waiting room for my exam.

I think the doctor was a little taken back by my progress. So much so that he said I could start using a walker. That wasn't supposed to occur for six more weeks. All I heard was I could start using a walker but that would come back to bite me.

I felt like I was "rode hard and put up wet" by the time we made it back to the ranch. It had been the best day I had in a long time. A good day will wear you out just as quickly as a bad day. All I wanted when we returned was a something to eat and a bed. I think I was asleep before my head hit the pillow.

No one thought anything about the fact that when they got up the next morning, they found me using the walker. The doctor had said it was time and the boys seemed happy for me. We had a good breakfast and they went to work. I don't think they thought much about me on the walker when they came home that evening.

The next morning I was awakened by the worst pain I believe I have ever felt. All the muscles in both of my legs were cramping. I guess I cried out a little louder than I thought because directly everyone came running into my room.

"What's wrong?" Brian asked in a concerned voice.

"My legs, my legs, I can't get to the bathroom," I cried out in pain.

They helped me, or should I say, carried me to the bathroom. Brian was scared half to death. Jon and JJ were still gone and he was in charge.

Finally it hit Garrett. He said, "Bill how long did you use your walker yesterday?"

"All day" was about all I could get out through a wave of pain.

"You old fool. The doctor said only a hundred steps a day. I guess you didn't hear that part, did you?" The boy questioned me like a seasoned lawyer - and not one on my side.

Garrett was right. I hadn't heard the hundred steps part. I considered myself a fine racehorse the day before. Perhaps even the second coming of Secretariat. A day later, I was feeling like a rundown old plug.

It wasn't just a one-day deal either. I was down for three days. Jon and JJ weren't just real happy with me when they got home that evening. Then Jon went outside and saw the new brush guard I had put on his truck and all was forgiven.

The new brush guard was just my way of thanking them for all they had done for me. They had gone far and beyond the call of duty. The brush guard didn't even come close but it was the least I could do.

I learned to pace myself even though I didn't like it. Day by day, I felt like I was getting better and day by day, Jon and JJ began to take the training wheels off. In reality, they had no choice.

The horse-show season was about to hit its stride. It was all hands on deck and that meant the boys would not be around as much. I would have the run of the place but it was also sink-or-swim time for me. "Could I completely take care of myself?" was the question that had to be answered.

The Youth World Paint Horse Show would prove to be my proving ground. The boys were needed in Fort Worth to help with the booths. Jon and JJ had purchased a saddle company and JJ and her mother were running a horse rehab service. Two booths manned twelve to fourteen hours a day required bodies and the bodies belonged to Garrett and Brian.

I had my daily hour visits by my nurses and therapists. I still had Jean and Rick, who were just down the road, and my buddy Zach just around the bend. So you can see help was close by if it was needed. I also had access to an ATV so I wasn't just stuck knocking around the big house by myself.

I made good use of that ATV from the very start of my home-alone phase of my recovery. The first morning I took it to Ramona's house. It was high time I thank her for the Hoverounds. I hadn't seen much of her since they had been delivered.

The next morning, I took it a little further. I went over to Rick and Jean's for breakfast. It had been awhile since I had a good sit-down breakfast and not one out of a bag. Things at a working horse ranch are pretty fast paced. So I savored every single bite with Rick and Jean.

On the third day I ventured even further. It was a little over three miles around the bend to Zach's place. I thought what the hell, a little male bonding never hurt anyone. You might say I was having a Tim Allen moment.

I knew where I would find Zach before I ever left the ranch. I have known Zach Terry since 1979 and he has been a gear head since I have known him. It made perfect sense to me when I heard he was teaching auto shop two decades ago.

"What else would the ratchet turning nut be doing?" I have often thought.

The only reason I stopped by his house that morning was to say hello to Jo, his wife. I knew before I ever knocked on the front door that Zach wasn't inside. I would find my friend where I had always found him: in the shop tinkering with his beloved jeeps. I don't think there has been a time in the boy's life that didn't own at least one. He showed up the first day of college in a 76 Jeep pick-up.

The boy was right where I knew he would be, doing exactly what I thought he'd be doing. We spent the better part of that morning rehashing our college days, talking cars and other stuff that two old men from the '70s talk about. It was fun, but of course it always is.

I left there realizing I had my independence back. I knew full well my days on the Double J Ranch were numbered. And that, my friend, was the best feeling of all.

CHAPTER 9

HOMECOMING

I felt like I was ready to go home two weeks before I did. I didn't want to seem ungrateful to my host. I think Jon was hoping I would move up there and said as much. Whitesboro just wasn't my home. The people of Whitesboro are friendly but they are not my people.

My mother and stepfather moved around so much that it was hard for the postal service to keep up with them. It is true, I call Aspermont my hometown but I didn't arrive there until the seventh grade. Five years later I was off to college.

When I was drinking, I was all over the country. As they say, "From sea to shining sea." I was always running from the same thing - myself. Who would have ever guessed I was so fast. Everywhere I went, there I was.

I guess the only regret in my life was all those years that my actions made my mother worry. The only good thing was I had been sober five years when she died. I still ought to have my ass kicked for the way I treated that beautiful lady.

I stopped my running in Lubbock, Texas. For some twelve years. With one wife and a slew of unhealthy relationships, I managed to pull my life together and I went back to school where I graduated with honors twice. I even bought two houses and fell into a rut.

I was teaching, going home and working on the houses day after day, right down to eating at the same place every day. I had my life together but my dreams went unfulfilled. Lubbock was a city and I was never a city person. While I did live there for twelve years, it never felt like home.

So what did I do? I did what I have always done best. I sold the houses and moved to the mountains with my last unhealthy relationship. Tammy was pretty, smart and had an education almost the equal to mine. She had only one problem: she couldn't leave the bottle alone.

Tammy, the girl I had nursed back to health numerous times, was dead in three months. She died alone in a motel room in the valley. She died with all her dreams unfulfilled. She died a death that could have been mine, if not for the Lord.

Her death showed me how short life really was. We all have a limited time on this round ball. What we do with that time is up to us. I didn't know what I wanted but I didn't want to leave this world with any unfulfilled dreams.

The Lord did something he has had a habit of doing all my life. He sent me an angel. My angel was a rough-talking, horse-loving Yankee named Amanda. I spoke earlier of her. She rekindled my love for horses and pushed me to take my writing to the next level. One year later I was on my first book tour.

The spring leg of my first book tour led me back to Texas. I figured if I couldn't sell cowboy books in Texas, I needed a new dream.

Sell I did - barnstorming my way through the Lone Star state. My writing career was taking off like a rocket. Newspapers were sparing no ink when it came to the "traveling cowboy storyteller."

Still I felt like something was missing. I didn't know what until I met another angel sent by the good Lord. If you have read any of my novels, you've read the name Susan Hairrell. It appears on the first page of every book. And if you read this book, you've seen her name several times. Susan is an angel sent by the Lord as well as my best friend.

This angel showed me a piece of heaven named Wise County and I fell in love with it, as well as all the other nuts who call it home. Now, for the first time in my life, I have found a place I can call home and have for going on sixteen years. I will die here and like old Bob Kurtz did and you can spread my ashes here.

I guess by now you figured out why I told Jon why I wouldn't leave my home. It was something he didn't take well. I hope after reading this part, he can understand what I have tried so many times to tell him. But like I said a few pages back, looking through the eyes of a 55-year-old is a lot different from seeing the world through the eyes of someone twenty years younger.

The Youth Paint World Show was nearly over but it was just the first in a long line of large horse shows. The next World Show was ten days off in Tunica, Mississippi. It is where I had my day in the sun a year earlier. There would not be a repeat, not this year anyway.

Jon and JJ have won this show nearly every year. I knew they were going this year as well, Jon had even asked me if I wanted to go. But Mississippi was a bridge too far with a broken pelvis. There was only one place I wanted to go and that was home. I wasn't going to spend the next two weeks alone on the Double J. I just didn't know how I was going to tell them.

JJ had come home for a bit of a breather the night before. I was already in bed by that time. Brian's wife and kids were with her or I would have gotten up and told her I wanted to go home. I knew they were headed back to Fort Worth the next day so I had a limited time to pick my spot.

The next morning I heard JJ in the kitchen and I knew it was then or never. Before I could get a word out, she was telling me what I wanted to tell her

"Bill, you have been on your own most of the week and you seem to be doing fine. Why don't you get in contact with the Home Health Care where you live? We are leaving in about a week and a half for Tunica and that ought to give you enough time to set everything up," I couldn't have said it any better myself.

The only thing was I didn't need a week and a half. But I felt like it was better coming out of her mouth and not mine. The last thing I wanted was to burn a bridge. I love Jon and JJ too much for that. They had done so much for me after the wreck. They fed and clothed me and then JJ gave me what I wanted most - going home with her blessing.

Like I said, I didn't need a week and a half. A cell phone and a few hours were all that were required. With any kind of luck I'd be sleeping in my own bed that night. I had already contacted the Home Health Care people.

The only thing left to do was pack and put in a call to the Saint of Cottondale. Kaz had already done so much for me, and I kind of felt guilty about asking to come get me but I did anyway. That's how bad I wanted to go home.

Big, old, lovable teddy bear Mike said he was more than happy to come get me. It would take him a few hours to get up there but he said he didn't mind. I think they were just as happy that I was coming home as I was - even after I told him about the two Hoverounds that needed to be loaded.

The next call I made was to my best friend Susan. I had already told her I wanted to come home but I was actually doing it. I was so happy I just wanted to share it with her. She was on her way back from the coast, so we joked about who was going to get home first.

I started packing for the long awaited ride home after the two calls were made. No, I was still mainly in a wheelchair so it wasn't an easy task. Packing my things took no time at all.

I had time to spare so I started moving everything to the front room. It didn't seem good enough so I moved everything outside. Garrett came in from the barn when I was trying to pull off that maneuver.

"You impatient so and so. You never can wait on anyone to help. You are going to jack around and end up in bed for three days like you did a few weeks ago," the boy preached to me.

I felt like saying, "You might be right but at least it will be my own bed," but I didn't. Instead I said, "I know, but just give me a hand and I will be out of your hair in no time at all."

After that little chore was done, all there was to do was to wait. I became real fidgety. Garrett was right. I have never been a patient person. It's just not in my nature.

I paced the best as I could while I waited for Mike. Garrett laughed at me the whole time. By and bye I saw Mike pull into the drive. I jumped up on my walker and went to greet my ride home. Garrett was right behind me to catch me if I fell but there would be no falling that day.

It wasn't no time at all before we had my things loaded and I was on my way home. It was two months to the day since I had left home for a roping - two months filled with life and death but most of all deep friendships. The bad days at the rest home were merely a distant memory. I was going home and that was all that mattered.

Z was waiting at the gate when we pulled in. It was almost like she knew the old man was coming home. I had to wipe the tear from my eyes before Mike could help me out of the truck.

I saw a truck driving in behind us. It was Jeremy, another one of my neighbors. I hadn't seen Jeremy since he and his wife had visited me in the hospital, the day Bobby Deane showed up. He and Mike had been sharing the critter-feeding duties. I have the best neighbors in the world, hands down.

The first thing Jeremy did after he dismounted his work truck was to go get Tater out of the kennel. He knew, without a shadow of a doubt, how to make my day. I have had Tater longer than any critter on the place.

"Now are you happy?" Jeremy fired in my direction.

"Happy hell, this is the best day I have had since my divorce was final," I joked the way men do when there are no ladies around. "The only way I'd be any happier if I had my pipe," I added.

I guess that was all it took. Mike disappeared into the house and returned with a pipe I had lost six months earlier and a pouch of tobacco. Don't ask me how he found it in a matter seconds. Like I said before, he is the Saint of Cottondale, I guess he has certain powers us mere mortals do not have.

I told myself, and anyone who would listen, that I had stopped smoking and I had for two months. But seeing what Mike had found, I fell off the wagon. I gave up whisky when I moved to Lubbock. I gave up wild women when I left Lubbock. My snuff dipping was history after meeting Susan. I have but one vice left and I am keeping it.

It wasn't long after that, Mike's and Jeremy's wives joined us in my front yard. It was then that I thanked everyone for holding down the fort while I was gone. I guess it was then I thought of the idea how to thank everyone. I would do it the Texas way. I would have a cookout in their honor.

Emily agreed she would take me to the store the next day. That was a good thing because the cupboard was bare at my place and I hadn't yet started back driving. Jeremy's wife Patty offered to give my house a good cleaning. Did I tell you what good neighbors I have? I guess I did but it deserves repeating.

The next morning, after a good night's sleep in my own bed, I got in my golf cart and went next door. Emily had offered to make me breakfast the night before. We were going to Wally World for a little shopping.

I asked her if we could make a few stops along the way. I didn't want to spring it on her like I had done Garrett a few weeks earlier.

We went to some of the same places Garrett and I had gone, like the bank and the post office. Then I told her I would like to go to the vet clinic where Susan worked. I hadn't seen Susan since my birthday, and I hadn't seen anyone at the clinic since before my wreck. Emily agreed and we were off.

All work at the clinic seemed to stop when we walked in. The lady working the front desk went to the back and told everyone I was there. Dr. Speed was the first to come out. She gave me a big hug and by the time she was through, there was Sheri (not to be confused with the other two in this book) and Mandy, both waiting for a hug. At the end of the line was my best friend. I hugged her like there was not going to be another hug.

By then Dr. Jim was in the lobby. He and I had become pretty good friends since Susan began working at the clinic. Every time we would talk on the phone, she would tell me Dr. Jim had asked about me. Dr. Jim's concerns really said something to me about the kind of man he is, even though he went to OSU. Hey, I had to throw in at least one jab.

I met with the Home Health Care people on my second full day home. I explained to them that I really didn't need a nurse or an aid. By that time I could pretty much take care of myself. What I did need was a therapist. What is the old saying, "Ask and you shall receive?"

I met my new therapist on the fourth day of my homecoming. Ronnie was every bit the man for the job. I would say he was cut from the same cloth as Bill Snow, the therapist I had as a child. He was hardnosed and direct to the point and like me a fan of Chris LeDoux. What more could you ask for?

The wheelchair and the walker soon took up residence in the barn. I was walking within a month of his arrival and back to work within six weeks. Thanks to Ronnie, I walked into my second doctor's appointment.

I don't think the good doctor could believe his eyes. It was thought that I wouldn't walk for six months, if at all. I guess they didn't know me - or Ronnie. Ronnie said I was different from most of his clients because I actually wanted to get better. I suppose that made the difference. Once again Martha Jane's boy had the grit to finish the fight.

The Fourth of July came and went without fan fair. But it wasn't the Fourth that I was looking forward to - it was the fifth. You see the fifth was the day of my big cookout. I wanted to make it special for everyone who had helped with my recovery. It started out being for the neighbors and grew from there.

The day before I had mounted my lawn mower and mowed the place. I couldn't walk but I could mow. It felt good to do something such as that for myself.

Mike stayed up all night smoking the meat. Shelly came over to vacuum and mop. Emily and Patty did the beans and the potato salad. Like my recovery, this fifth of July cookout was a group effort. Right down to the deviled eggs made famous by Susan and the dessert delivered by Dr. David Lowe. It was a feast.

You might ask what Jeremy and I did? Well I bought the beer, even though I do not drink. You cannot have an old-fashioned Texas cookout without beer. And as far as Jeremy is concerned, he drank the beer, because Jeremy does drink.

Not everyone who had helped me along the path of recovery could be there. Jon and JJ had gone to Tunica for the horse show. A lot of people were out of town for the Fourth of July. I had only met Ronnie a few days before. I think I did invite him but he had other plans.

Sherri had gone to see her grand babies but she did put in an appearance four hours after the deal wrapped up. Sherri had been to my place at least three times before. I just figured she knew how to get there. What I didn't know is she had gone high tech.

I love that woman with all my heart but sometimes she can have a blonde moment. Instead of relying on her memory to come to my place, she relied on her GPS. Well sometimes it works and sometimes it doesn't. That night, it didn't.

I received a frantic call from the prettiest woman to ever come out of Oklahoma about an hour before dark. (I thought I'd better say that after the crack about her being a blonde.)

"Bill, I cannot find your place. I am mad, tired and almost out of gas. I just want go home," she said sounding like she was nearly in tears.

"Sherri, you have been out here before - what is wrong?" I knew as soon as I said it. It was the last thing I should have said.

"It's this stupid GPS. It tells me to turn left, turn right. I have been going around in circles for hours." She said and by then I think she was in tears.

"Turn the damn thing off and tell me where you are," I told her. Come to find out, she was but a mile or so from my place. "I am going to take the golf cart and meet you at the end of the road. Just look for the crippled guy on the Flintstone mobile."

I explained it that way because that is what my 30-year-old golf cart looks like. Both of us kind of stick out.

It wasn't long before she found me - or I found her depending who you asked. She followed me back to the house while the onlookers thought we were crazy.

Despite the fact that Sherri had spent an hour as lost as an Easter egg, we had a pretty good visit. I hadn't seen her since the night the tornado almost got us at the old folks' home. She and her mother had spent the weekend cooking up a bunch of food for me that was the reason for the visit.

I had the food left over from the cookout, plus the food she had brought from her mother's. It was plain to see that I wasn't going to starve. That's not counting the fact the neighbors brought by a plate every night and they still do. I guess everyone is bound and determined to put some weight on these skinny bones.

I thought about the day. I even thought about all the folks I wanted to be a part of my party that couldn't make it. It was a good day and I had to thank the Lord for giving me such a day. What I didn't know was it was only a sign of what lay in store for me. There was a storm brewing in the Fort Worth Stockyards.

"Ladies and Gentlemen. Wild Bill, who recently was in a very bad car wreck, has just entered the exhibit hall," Paula announced on the PA system my first day back at work. Her words nearly made me cry. I don't know if you have noticed, but I am doing a lot of crying in this book. What can I say? I am just an old softy since the wreck.

The NCHA Summer Cutting in Fort Worth is where I chose to make my comeback. It seemed only fitting since the Fort Worth cuttings were the first horse shows I ever did. You might say my roots run deep in the cutting-horse world and my friendships run even deeper.

They had all heard or read about my little crack up. I had even received cards, letters and contributions from these wonderful people when I was at the old folks' home. Everyone greeted me with open arms in the exhibit hall.

Cindy and Art come to mind and by all rights they should. They are two of the sweetest people you'd every wish to meet. Come to think of it, Art was the first person I saw when I arrived. I was in the underground parking trying to unload the Hoveround by myself. I still wasn't in the best of shape.

"Hey Bill, let me give you a hand," I heard from behind me. I turned to find there was good ole Art. I wasn't going to argue with the man because I had been fighting with the thing for some time.

I was rolling down the alleyways of vendors in no time at all. I received all kinds of handshakes and pats on the back. First it was Mark and Tony, two hat makers. Then came the crusty ole saddle maker Kenny Kerns. It felt good to be around my people at last. The cutting world is like one big family -

maybe at times a dysfunctional family but a family nonetheless.

I was on my way to the arena when I was stopped by Cindy, Art's wife. She handed me a check and said it came from God. Maybe it did come from the Lord, but one of his earthly angels had delivered it and it was written on her account.

I made my way to the arena after I got the lump out of my throat from Cindy's kind actions. I wanted to see a little of what I termed "The Cutter's Dance." I couldn't watch it from the lower deck like I should of. I had to be where the action was.

The upper level is where the trainers go to watch the cows. It is also where Tom the announcer resides. To get to where I wanted to go, I had to go up a flight of cement steps. I knew it would be tricky at best. Then I remembered the chairlift on the other side.

I had seen Chubby Turner use it a few years back when his leg was busted when a colt rolled on him. If it was good enough for Chubby it was good enough for me. Now if Chubby was only around to show me how to operate the lift. I guess that would be too much to ask for.

Chubby may not have been there but the before-mentioned Tom was. Tom helped me get loaded into the contraption then skyward I went in the chairlift. I received a hero's welcome once I breached the summit. There, low and behold sat Chubby not ten feet away from me.

"And you made fun of me when I had to use that damn thing," the old horse trainer said with a laugh. He had me there is all I have to say.

You might say I saved the best for last. There was only one person left to see after I watched a set of cows. Of all the people I know in the cutting world, Tiffani Banuelos has to be my favorite. It might have a little to do with her being the prettiest woman in the cutting world, and her beauty is inside and out.

I can still remember the day I met Tiff even though it has been nearly twenty years ago. It was a cold December evening at my first cutting event. I was working the barns with my first book. I was on my last barn and then I was going back to the exhibit hall to get warmed up. All of a sudden I saw this beautiful blonde, she was spitting out Mexican words better than most Mexicans.

We talked for a good while that evening and we have been good friends ever since. Every time I go to a cutting, I have to find my Tiffani. It has been one of my pleasures watching her three children grow into world-class cutters. I can't tell you how many times I have eaten with the whole family and laughed.

After I said all this, I'm sure you understand why I had to find her that day. Tiff is not the easiest person to find sometimes but I had my heart set on it. It took awhile but I got the job done. Tiff had just heard about the wreck so she was just as happy to see me as I was seeing her.

All in all, it was one of my happiest days at a cutting, my dear friends saw to that. I left Will Rogers with a bunch of new memories - memories I will take to my grave. I guess that is why I did my best to honor these dear people in this section of the book.

My homecoming, from the day Kaz came and picked me up to my first day back at work were some of the best days of my life. But the good Lord wasn't done yet. The best was yet to come.

CHAPTER 10

A BIG BALL IN COW TOWN

I don't know when I started writing but I do know it was over a broken heart in high school. I got my start writing love songs and for a young boy, I was pretty good at it. I even had one of my songs sung at homecoming one year. I was high as a $100 kite when my friend finished the tune. I did not win the girl's heart but I did cast my future.

It seemed no matter how bad things got, I always had my writing. At 24, I moved to Eastland, Texas. This is where I honed my song-writing skills as well as my beer-drinking skills. I became the writer and light man for a local rock group called Party Line.

July 4, 1985, I was making a beer run for the band. I turned the radio on just in time to hear a song I had written. I damn near wrecked the car when I heard it. I drank a lot of beer in my day but nothing ever topped hearing a Wild Bill-composed song on the radio.

I guess hearing my song on the radio, gave me the bright idea to move to Nashville. Two things seemed to conspire against me: my drinking and the fact that everyone in Nashville is a songwriter. I am talking about from the milkman to the checkout clerk at Safeway.

You might say my hair-brained idea was doomed from the start. So with my tail between my legs, I jumped aboard a redeye flight back to Texas. There was something about free booze on a plane that was so alluring. I was drunker than Cooter Brown by the time the Southwest flight touched down in Lubbock.

I am proud to say that was the last running drunk I was ever on. Like I wrote earlier, I got my act together in Lubbock. I packed away my dreams of becoming a songwriter and joined the human rat race. I was doing just fine until my beer-drinking idol came out with a book.

Jimmy Buffett had written a book of short stories and my adopted little sister, Sherri, bought me a copy for my thirty-first birthday. She knew what a fan I was of this modern-day Key West pirate. The book set my world on its ear.

It was so simple what Jimmy had done. He had taken the songs off his latest record and turned them into short stories. Well I am a bit of a pirate myself. I stole his concept. Within a couple of weeks, using one of my songs as an outline, I composed my first short story and gave birth to my favorite character Bubba Lee.

It was a time before PC's were affordable so I did all my writing on a typewriter. The writing I did back then was mainly for me so it didn't matter what I wrote it on. Nashville had already crushed one dream and I wasn't ready to make it two.

The next year I set sail with Bubba Lee again in my first full-length book. What I didn't know at the time was that it was destined to be a twenty-year voyage. **Captain Cowboy** was the first book I ever wrote but it was like the fourteenth that I released. It was my baby and I wanted it to be perfect.

The first book I released was kind of like Buffett's first book. It was composed of four short stories taken from my songs and a number of my songs themselves. By then I was calling them poems. From there it was off to the races with my writing career.

Early on in my new career as a writer I traveled this great land of ours, mainly the Great Northwest. It was on one of these summer-long tours that I came face to face with my hero, the legendary Chris LeDoux. Chris was everything I thought he would be and more.

To my surprise he had already heard of me. You see I had left a book for him the year before. I never dreamed he would actually read the thing. You talk about walking on air, purified by the great cowboy himself. That made my whole summer worth it.

Later on that summer, I was driving down highway 59 in Wyoming. I had just bought a new Chris LeDoux CD. Now friends, there is nothing on that hundred-mile stretch of black top.

Chris, if he was nothing else, was one of the best storytellers there ever was. The song, ***The Yellow Outlaw Stud*** came through my speakers, and blew me away.

If there was ever a song that needed to be turned into a novel, Chris had penned it. I had the thing written in my head before I ever stopped for gas. The plan was to go back home, write the book and surprise Chris with it the following year.

I'm sad to say that Chris LeDoux didn't have the following year. He left us way too young but I made sure his wife, Peggy, had a copy. I delivered it myself.

The book went on the market at the right time and went to number one in Wyoming, as did the follow-up book, ***Life is a Highway***. The last in the trilogy was ***Old Songs and Memories***. By then I had too many critters to drive all over the Great Northwest.

The writer in me had evolved. Not only was I turning my own songs into stories, I was turning other folks' works into books. My next victim was found in the most well-known little town in Texas: Luckenbach. It was there I met Thomas Michel

Riley. Through that chance encounter, I wrote, *Perfectly Normal*. It was written by using one of Tommy's songs as my blue print.

Through Tommy I met everyone who is anyone on the Texas music scene. These entertainers soon became some of my closest friends. Mike Blakely, singer, songwriter and novelist writer to the stars, became the big brother I never had.

Suddenly I was traveling in the same circles as the top songwriters and performers in the Lone Star state. It took me thirty years but I am where I always wanted to be. Who needs Nashville? I should have learned that from Willie.

I remember the first time I met Tommy Alverson. I was with Blakely and Brian Burns, another Texas song-writing giant. I had agreed to meet them at the Tommy Alverson Family Gathering, a Texas music festival held every year. I had no idea who the hell Tommy Alverson was.

We were all talking and joking around when this little crazy guy shows up on a golf cart. I mean I thought the dude was the coolest. He was nuts but he was damn sure cool.

"Who the hell was that?" I asked when the man drove off.

"He's our host; that's Tommy Alverson," Blakely answered.

Tommy and I have become good friends ever since that first meeting. I have been to every Family Gathering for some thirteen years. If the Good Lord is willing, I'll be at the next one in a few weeks. When I sat down and rewrote **Captain Cowboy**, I made a spot for Tommy in the book.

I really didn't grasp how good of friends Tommy and I were until the wreck. I had heard the rumor about all my friends in the music industry wanting to put together a Benefit for me when I was on the Double J Ranch. Pete, the craziest man I know, had let it slip on the phone one day.

It was a wonderful thought that really touched me, but I never dreamed it would really happen. It was in the middle of the summer, the busiest time of year for musicians. The people I knew in the music world were scattered all over God's green earth.

One day I received another call from crazy man Pete.

"Tommy wants your address. He has four big shows he is doing. He says he's going to pass around the hat to help you with the bills until he can put the Benefit together," Pete informed me.

The passing of the hat has become a time-tested tradition in Texas. Its purpose is to help friends or loved ones in a time of need. I gave Pete my address after I had choked back a few tears.

I put in a call to Blakely after I returned to my place. I wanted to know if he had heard anything about the Benefit.

"Yes I heard the rumor," my dear friend told me. "I told Alverson not to do anything until I can clear a date for it. It's a party I am not about to miss. If you need any more information call Gary Newell."

Musicians are a lot like book writers - they are not very organized. That is the reason why I have Susan and Sherri and that is why Tommy has his wife, Amy, and Gary Newell.

I needed to talk to Gary anyway. The best vehicle I ever owned was sitting in some junkyard, God knows where. I had sold the Town Car and all I had left was my ranch truck. Believe me when I tell you, it looks like it's been through the ringer.

Gary might be the best auto body man in North Texas. That is when he's not helping to keep Alverson organized. I told him I had an old truck in need of a facelift and could he come look at it when he had time. I was still able to drive or I would have taken it to him.

He agreed to come out and look at the truck and we could talk about the other deal when he arrived. He did assure me that the Benefit was still on. They wanted to make sure I could attend and they could get on the same page with Blakely.

I told him I'd have to be in another coma to miss my own benefit. Blakely, well that was a whole different kettle of fish. Sometimes musicians are a lot like herding cats. I said I would call the boy and try to light a fire under him.

Alverson had already beaten me to the punch. When I called Blakely, he informed me they had a date set and all we needed was a venue. By that time I wanted to be involved in the scheme of things. I told Mike, Gary and I would figure it out.

A few days later, Gary drove out to have a look at my beat-up ranch truck. He inspected my old bucket of bolts and told me it was fixable but it might take a while to run down the parts. I assured him the thing wasn't going anywhere.

Our conversation then went to the Benefit. I told him what Blakely had said about the date and the venue. Gary said he would talk to the owner of the Longhorn Saloon in the Fort Worth Stock Yards. He then asked me if any of the vendors I knew from the horse shows would donate to the action they wanted to have at the Benefit. I saw my opening to get involved.

"Gary, I don't know what the protocol is for a Benefit, or your own Benefit, but I want to help. I have never been one to sit on the sidelines. I am no good at watching from afar," I explained to my friend.

"Bill, I don't think there are any protocols. If there are I don't know them. We have three weeks to pull this thing together. I would say, it's all hands on deck," the man told me.

It was all Gary had to say to me, I hit the ground running. The first thing, and more than likely the best thing I did, was enlist my Sherri. She told me when I first heard the rumor that she wanted to do something. Believe me, we found plenty for her to do.

My next call was to a pair of crazy DJ's well known in our music circle. Carry Dean and Nash have a morning show on the radio. These two nuts have been making me laugh for years. I figured it was high time someone gave them a real job.

They had heard about the wreck as well as the Benefit. I guess Facebook leaves no one behind but me. What can I say, I like my flip phone. They wanted in on the deal, so I told them to call Alverson. This was Tommy's ship and I didn't want to go behind his back with anything. I wasn't raised to show gratitude in that manner.

I put them in touch with Sherri after Tommy gave the thumbs up on my deal. Let me say this before I go any further. This was a group effort with Tommy at the helm, or should I say Amy and Gary. I think Amy outworked us all. You see I was also taught to give credit where it is due.

Between Sherri and the on-air twins, they enlisted another friend of ours. Ed has been known to fry fish anywhere, at the drop of a hat.

"What would be a summer get together be without a fish fry?" is how Ed's wife, Sharla, put it to me.

Who was I to argue with such logic? I left for a horse show in Tulsa after I had my troops lined out, or should I say Amy's. It was high time I got some work done myself. Clay with Cowboy Bronze donated a crystal sculptor for the action while I was there.

I had no sooner made it home before I had to leave again to go to a ranch rodeo. I made some haul for the auction at this event. I really don't want to leave anyone out here, but if I do, please forgive me. I would like to thank Rod, Peggy, the two Matts, the happy toy maker and the prettiest red head in Texas for their contributions for the auction.

We had a week to go before the Big Ball in Cow Town by the time I made it home. I think I spent the whole week on the phone. I called everyone I knew to invite them to the Ball. By then it was billed as Wild Bill's Wild Benefit.

I was as nervous as a long-tailed cat in a room full of rocking chairs before the big day. I was scared to death I would show up and be the only one there, just like my first memory in the coma. I don't know where the feelings were coming from so I kept them to myself.

Each night I was on the phone with Sherri. I guess she could tell how nervous I was so she asked if I could pick her up the morning of the Ball. She also wanted to know what size hat I wore.

I kind of laughed to myself. "It depends if anyone shows up or not. If they do, I'm going to need a really big hat," I thought to myself but didn't say out loud.

I didn't sleep real well the night before the big bash. That is kind of the norm for me anyway. I have never been able to sleep before big event. The event the following day just might be the biggest of my life.

All my friends, from all walks of life were coming to honor and help me. Why wouldn't it be the biggest day of my life? The only other time I could think something like this could happen would be at my wake.

The next day I even told Blakely, "It's kind of like being at your own funeral."

Mike just laughed and called me Huck Finn, knowing full well how much I love Mark Twain. I can't rightly remember if it was Huck or Tom, but one of them went to their own funeral.

I was up and ready before the clock struck 9 a.m. I had never been to Sherri's house before so I allowed myself enough time to find it. I am not like her, I do not have GPS and after the deal she went through getting to my house, I don't know if I want one.

I saw Gordon's truck in the old IGA parking lot as I drove through town. Gordon was one of the first people I remember seeing when I woke up from the coma.

"I wonder if I told Gordon about the Benefit?" I asked myself as I went by. I had a course, but that morning I was too scatter brained to remember it.

I had to get some gas. I told myself that if his truck was still there when I finished, I would go find him. Sure enough his truck was still there after I paid for my gas. I turned my truck around and headed to where I knew I would find him.

The town of Boyd isn't that big, and on Sunday morning there is hardly a soul about. It came as little surprise to me that Gordon was the first person I ran into at the store.

"You are leaving pretty early if it starts at 2," is how my old friend greeted me.

"I have to go over to North Fort Worth and pick up my date, then we are going to go help them set up. You are coming, right?" I asked him.

"I told you I was. I wouldn't miss it," Gordon assured me.

With Gordon's assurance in hand, I lit out for Sherri's place. She had given me the directions the night before. I was doing fine until I hit a highly populated area in the rich part of town. I remember everyone just looking at my beat-up old truck like "What is this fool doing over here?"

"If you think this one looks bad, you ought to see my last vehicle," I felt like saying.

I waited until the last minute before I called Sherri. She talked me through it until I saw this cute blonde standing in the yard talking on her cell. X marked the spot so I whipped the old ranch truck into her drive.

"We better hurry up and go before someone thinks I am robbing you," I said pointing at the wreck I had driven up in.

"Don't worry, I'll just tell them you're here to do yard work," Sherri fired back. "Come in the house I have something for you," she then ordered.

"Are you sure someone will not swipe my truck?" I couldn't resist one last joke.

Once inside, Sherri presented me with a new shirt and a palm-leaf cowboy hat. Then she started dressing me like I was a small lad. I guess once a mother, always a mother.

I thanked her for her kindness and we talked a little before we headed out. I did get even with her for the yard work crack she made. You see I made her drive that beat-up old truck while I rode shotgun.

Alverson was unloading his truck as we pulled in behind him. I could not wait to get out of the truck to see my old friend. It had been sometime since I had seen him. Getting out of my truck is easier said than done. You see the passenger side door will not open. I told you it was a wreck.

I gave Tommy a big hug once I made it out of my very own sinking ship. Amy came up behind me, and she gave me another hug. Then I heard this voice yelling behind me, "Get your crippled ass out of the street." I turned to find Carry Dean, one of the on-air twins had pulled up behind me.

"At least I am not a freaking midget. They are not shooting a remake of the Wizard of Oz today," I fired back. This is just Carry Dean's and my way of saying, "I love you man."

Sherri then pointed out the picture of me on the billing. Below my likeness it read, "Wild Bill's Wild Benefit" I guess that is what brought it all home to me. This was the reason that I was there. I was there on the threshold of my greatest day because my friends loved me. If that will not choke a person up, I do not know what will.

It wasn't long before we had my truck unloaded including the Hoveround. I debated rather or not to bring the thing. I knew it was going to be a long day and so I opted for a little help if I needed it.

I had never been to the Longhorn Saloon before, even though I bet I walked past it a hundred times over the years. The place was really a class act from the staff to the owner. I would like to thank all those from the Longhorn who made everyone feel at home and a special thanks goes out to the owner who let us use the place.

Tyla was the first one of my adopted family to show up. I wasn't real sure she was going to make it. She had concerns about the smoke that you often find in bars. Tyla was carrying her first child and was not taking any risk. I just heard the other day it was going to be a little girl. Susan is going to make a great grandmother.

From my vantage point, I saw her and her husband walk in. This is where I moved into protective action. I took the reserve sign off of my table and seated Tyla and her husband in the far corner. I put the Reserve sign on their table because I knew the rest of the family would be along.

The next people I remember seeing was Blondie and his family from Aspermont, Texas. We had grown up together. He had driven all the way from the coast. I hadn't seen him in a few years but I had talked to him on the phone when I was laid up in the hospital. His sister is Nancy, a lady mentioned many times in this book. I put them at the table next to Tyla because I knew none in their party smoked.

It was about that time the floodgates opened. I really can't say who I talked to next. My memory is good but it's not that good. People came from all the different stages of my life. One of my Fraternity brothers from college and Dr. Lowe represented good ole E.T.S.U. well.

Jon and JJ were there. They represented part of my horse family. Every single member of the Hairrell family was there as were most of the Rogers clan. It was like a family reunion and it was like no other.

I can't begin to tell you how many from the music world attended or from my horse-show vendor world. Before I knew it, the place was packed, as Blakely would say, "From brim to brim." And just think, I was worried that no one would show up.

Sherri grabbed me when the music started. "I want to dance," she told me. Dancing was the one thing I hadn't counted on. I wasn't real sure I could but I gave it the ole college try. I wasn't half bad if I do say so myself.

Seeing that I could cut a rug gave Sherri another idea. She disappeared for a minute when I wasn't looking. I figured she had gone to the ladies room. Directly she did come back, smiling ear to ear. I knew something was up. I just didn't know if it was good or bad.

"Bill I just talked to the DJ and he has some Chris LeDoux songs. Why don't you go pick us one out and we will dance to it when Tommy and the guys take a break." She didn't have to tell me twice.

I picked out one of my favorite LeDoux love songs and one more just for good measure. She took my hand after the first set was over and we walked to the dance floor. "*Just Look At You Girl*," came the immortal words of the great Chris LeDoux.

It felt like the angel of the man himself had walked into my bash. I guess in a way he did. I had been close to death and I had heard my mother's voice but I hadn't seen heaven. As I danced with Sherri to my old friend's song, with all my friends and loved ones watching, I was almost certain I was getting a glance at the here ever after. I am surprised there was enough room to dance.

It seems like almost everyone brought something for the auction. A lot of them were high-ticket items. The Longhorn Saloon was starting to look like a redneck version of Walmart. That's without any Duck Commander products. All that was lacking were Amy and her Daisy Dukes. But we did have Big Earl and he's about as redneck as a redneck gets.

There were enough items that we could have had two auctions. So that is exactly what we did. We had a live action and a silent auction. During the live auction, Sherri became the main attraction. She reminded me of the Price is Right girls as she displayed every item.

The night ended way too soon, I wish it could have lasted forever and not because I was the headliner and not because of the nearly $13,000 that was raised. It was special because of the love that filled that ole honky tonk.

It was special not because I was there, but because most of the people I love were there. It was a time to sing and dance, it was a time to laugh and it was a time to celebrate friendship. In short it was a night like no other.

I would like to close this chapter by thanking everyone who came and making the day amazing for me. There is no way I could mention everyone by name but my memory just isn't that good.

I would like to thank everyone who helped put the thing on. Without you, this night would have never have happened. My dearest memory would have never been made. My day in the sun was truly a special one.

I would also like to think all those who performed. You guys took time out of your day to come put on one hell of a show. Nashville would have been jealous if it would have been televised. So thanks Tommy, Mike, Jeff, Steve, Ed, Brian and whoever else went to the stage and made it what it was.

And thanks to all the little people. Wait a minute there was only one there. I am just playing Carry Dean, I love you man!

CHAPTER 11

FULL CIRCLE

It was an eventful summer, I'll give you that. A summer only experienced because of the grace of God. By all rights, I should have died in that wreck. I know it and everyone who came to see me in those early days knows it as well.

When I first sat down to write this book, I was going to call it, "***On a Dime***" because life can change on a dime. Mine did in early May. Some might say it took a turn for the worse but I just don't see it that way. I guess because I have a whole new understanding of life, one that I could not have found any other way.

Then I thought about calling the book "***Grace***" but that only tells half the story. As stated earlier I am still here because of God's Grace. I believe that to be true with all my heart. But there was something else, something besides the Lord's Grace.

The next title I came up with was "***Grace and Friendships***." I thought about that for a day before I decided against it. You see because of everything that has happened this summer, I see friendships differently. Then I almost settled on "***Grace and Earthly Angels***" as the title.

However, I don't think I would have ever made it without the love of my friends. There is no way to quantify the number of prayers or the number of people filling the good Lord's ears with those prayers when I lay between life and death.

That's when I settled on *"**Angels And Outlaws**."* This being Texas and all, I've known an assortment of outlaws during my life, but mostly the good kind and sometimes they can be one in the same.

However, I really discovered the "angels" in my life during those dark hours and while I was recuperating. Once the darkest of hours were behind me, it was the love of my friends and their actions that nursed me back to health.

An old cowboy once told me he was a millionaire. I looked at his scuffed-up boots, the holes in his jeans and the beat up truck he drove.

"How do you figure, George?" I asked trying my best not to laugh at the old timer.

"You see son, I reckon I have a million friends. I know if I asked each one for a dollar, they would give it to me," came the old man's drawn-out answer. Being a young and foolish kid, I thought the old coot had fallen off his horse one too many times.

A few years later, George was called to heaven's big roundup. The day of his funeral, my hometown swelled to three times its actual size. People from all over the country, even the Governor came to say their last goodbyes.

It was the largest funeral Aspermont had ever seen or will again. I thought I knew then what the old man was trying to tell me. I thought I knew again when I saw his picture hanging in the real Cowboy Hall of Fame.

But it was only knowing. Now I can honestly look toward the heavens and say, "Hey George, I am a millionaire too." It is just something this summer has taught me.

I see something different in the mirror from what I did in early May. Success is not about how much money I have made. It's not about how many books I have sold. It's not even about my station in life. To me success is about how many hearts I have touched and how many have touched mine.

I thought about the horse I was about to buy and the barn I was going to build as I drove to that roping in early May. I now have a horse and a new barn. It's not the horse I was going to get off the Waggoner Ranch and it's not a barn that looks like I am the one that built it.

Down the road at Jeremy's place, there lived this old chestnut gelding. I have wanted that horse ever since the first time I saw him. Two days before the big ball in Cow Town, Jeremy up and gave him to me.

Brad, another good friend of mine, came over and built me a real nice barn for cost. "Yes George, I am a millionaire."

I have come full circle since that day in May. I am walking and back to work. I might even be in better shape than I was before all this happened. I never stopped working out after reaching my goals. I doubt if I have been in this good of shape since high school.

I would like to leave you with one last thought. On my mother's headstone, the epitaph reads, "Martha Jane, Loved by all who knew her." It's very few words to describe one who lived but 53 years. Few words are not, bad. They capture who she really was.

I cannot make up for all the times I let her down and she would never ask me to. What I can do is live by the ways she taught me and perhaps when it's my time to go, they will say, "He was loved by all who knew him."

CPSIA information can be obtained
at www.ICGtesting.com
Printed in the USA
FFOW05n1621170716